This is a fascinating, emotional and excitin[...] [...] [...] As Fingerhut tells his story, he also shares tips and [...] [...] [...] to help you get a life full of extraordinary experiences.

Shep Hyken,
New York Times bestselling author of *The Amazement Revolution*

Finally, a book written in a way where students are engaged and inspired to succeed! Joe cares about students and the detailed stories in this book are examples of his passion for students.

Fabian Ramirez, National Youth Speaker

Joe is a talented author/speaker whose book *Permission to Play* will help both students and grownups set big goals and make their dreams happen.

Brooks Gibbs, CEO, Golden Rule School

"In *Permission to Play*, Joe pours his heart out and shares his timely knowledge. He puts it all out on the table for us. I am strongly confident that after reading this book, you will not need permission to play. You will be ready to play in all areas of your life. This book will encourage you let go of the stinkin' thinking and become the go-getter you are meant to be. I recommend this resource for teens everywhere!"

Laymon A. Hicks
Speaker | Author | Youth Leadership Strategist

Joe Fingerhut doesn't want life to be boring—not his, not yours, not anybody's! In the years I have known Joe, he stands out as a person committed to making life extraordinary. This book details Joes' approach to life, and how anyone can overcome the same excuses Joe had, in order to make extraordinary things happen in life. Joe's focus is teens, but as an author and coach for entrepreneurs, I can say he will help YOU to be inspired by life's opportunities and you will LOVE *Permission to Play*!

JT DeBolt, CEO of Mach I Strategies and Consulting

All too often, "Pursue your dreams" is a throwaway idea that we give to young people without any guidance or support. It sounds great, but to actually follow your dreams is daunting and overwhelming. Luckily, Joe has taken the guesswork out of the process. With clarity, understanding, and a ton of humor, he shares the stories that illustrate how to chase your dreams! I've known Joe for almost 20 years and no one walks the walk like him. It doesn't matter what age you are, if you are a student of life, you need to read this book.

David Fisher, speaker, author, and CEO of RockStar Consulting

Our work at the National Council on Alcoholism and Drug Abuse-St. Louis Area is about engaging young people to be leaders in their schools and communities. It can be difficult to have fun with youth and educate them on an important topic like substance abuse, but Joe is able to do it and make it look easy! Every time we work with Joe, our staff and the young people have a great time and walk away feeling inspired. Joe has been a part of NCADA activities for many years, we have loved watching him develop his message and we are never disappointed!

Jenny Armbruster, Director of Community Services, NCADA

Entertaining, Engaging and Most Meaningful are words I use to describe Joe's style. He has this extraordinary ability to keep everyone tuned into his presentation, which is packed with meaningful points and reflections that audiences of all levels enjoy.

Michael Teoh, Co-Author of *Potential Matrix* &
Malaysia's National Youth Icon

Teens need encouragement and inspiration, whether they are in America, Australia, or any country on earth. Joe's various adventures in different countries and life experiences in this book display his passion for not only pursuing big dreams, but providing a blueprint for others to pursure theirs. Permission to Play is a GREAT resource for people excited about pursuing adventure and loving their lives.

Simon Clegg, Top Youth Speaker in Australia and New Zealand

Permission to Play

*How Teens Can Build a Life
That is Fun, Fulfilling, and Promising*

To Molly —

by

Joe Fingerhut

Thank you for all your support over these many years.

Stay true to your dreams!

Joe Fingerhut

CONTENTS

PART I
DON'T SETTLE:
IF I BUILT A LIFE THAT'S FUN
AND FULFILLING, SO CAN YOU!

PART II
NO MORE EXCUSES:
HOW TO SLAY THE "I CAN'T" DRAGON,
SO YOU CAN GET WHAT YOU WANT

PART III
EXERCISES FOR INDIVIDUAL
OR GROUP STUDY

FOREWORD

You know what's really hard? Making yourself into who you want to be. Making your life into what you want it to be.

These things are really hard because you have to start where you're at, and where you're at is never the easy place to start.

Starting takes guts. It takes courage. It takes nerve. It takes real audacity to declare to the world that you're going to become what you dream and then go for it. Real audacity. And a touch of crazy. The good kind of crazy. The kind of crazy that shapes amazing lives.

Joe Fingerhut is that kind of person. He's done it. He's been though it. He's gotten the T-shirt. He's learned the power of dreaming. The magic of starting. The necessity of falling down. The all-importance of getting back up again and forging on.

But there's no need to be impressed with Joe's accomplishments. They're not why you should trust what he says in the pages of this book. Who cares what Joe's accomplished? Joe accomplished his dreams, not yours.

Instead, give applause to the number of times Joe has fallen, failed, crashed, burned, wiped out, screwed up, suffered, persisted, and overcome all to pursue his biggest dreams, because that's what gives Joe the depth to share real wisdom with you.

Joe rides a unicycle not because he can. Joe rides a unicycle because he dreamed of riding one, and then he fell down ten thousand times for over a year, learning to make his dream real.

Joe speaks around the world not because people invite him to. He speaks around the world because he dreamed of doing so and then gutted it out for years, doing whatever he could to become an international speaker.

I first met Joe when he was in college. I gave a talk at his University, and Joe stuck around to talk to me a bit afterward. The event was a spark of inspiration for Joe to live his dreams, especially his dream to become a speaker one day, like me.

Joe kept in touch with me a little bit over of the years. I received an email from him when he was teaching overseas. He updated me as his accomplishments as a DJ, juggler, and magician stacked up. But it wasn't until Joe shifted his focus to actually fulfill his dream to be a speaker that I really got to know him. I learned what makes Joe tick.

What makes Joe tick is something important for you and every human being to value. Joe values his family, and Joe values his dreams, and his life is a reflection of these two values. But underneath both of those values is something even more fundamental to Joe. Joe values life.

There is always something that drives each of us do what we do in life. Regrettably, too many people are driven by the desire to be comfortable, safe, or rich, and these people are chained to very boring lives.

Joe doesn't place the same kind of value on safety, comfort, or money that most people do. At the heart of Joe's life is a value for life itself because, as you'll read in this book, Joe learned at a young age, through a very painful loss, that life is precious and can be extinguished at any moment.

You hold in your hand an excellent manual on how to really live while you're alive, how to fill the pages of your own life story with play, joy, love, adventure, friendship, excitement, achievement, excellence and fulfillment. Read every page of this book.

But more importantly, do as Joe did. Be so crazy that you make yourself into who you want to be. Be so audacious that you make your life into what you dream. Why? Because you can. Because your life depends on it.

Live Brave,

Patrick Combs
New York City
June 2015

DEDICATION

To my parents, Joe and Julie. You both not only gave me life, but propelled me to build and love the life I have.

Part I

DON'T SETTLE:

If I Built a Life That's Fun and Fulfilling, So Can You!

CHAPTER 1

My Best Friend Died

"Joe, I don't know how to tell you this, but I have some bad news about Mark."

On the first day of kindergarten, I met my best friend. I saw him playing on the swings at the park across the street from my house. I thought he looked like a boy I had met at school that morning.

"Hey!" I yelled. "Are you in kindergarten at Corpus Christi? What's your name?"

"Mark Garvey!" he called back.

From that day forward, Mark and I had a brotherly bond. His family lived just around the corner, and Mark and I were inseparable. We were the same age, we were boys, and we always stirred up something.

We played every sport together at school. In soccer, Mark was the defensive leader as our goalie, and I was the offensive leader as a forward. In baseball, he was the catcher, and I was the shortstop. In basketball, Mark was the last guy off the bench, and I was the second-to-last guy off the bench. Or, sometimes, it was the other way around. His father coached baseball, my dad coached basketball, and my mom watched all four of the Garvey boys, as well as her own four kids, every day after school.

Eighth grade was our last year at Corpus Christi, our parish school, and our classmates and teammates enjoyed this final year together before we splintered off to different high schools. The basketball team had been together for six years, which meant that my dad had coached us since second grade. The eighth grade team featured a few new guys, as well as several of us who had been there from the beginning. At fourteen, the combination of our growth spurts and our long history together produced a lot of victories. Our past seasons had been decent, but everything came together in eighth grade when we became winners. We expected to win every game, and Dad entered us into eight tournaments that year. However, in the first three of those, we finished in second or third place because we lost to our archrival, St. Norbert's.

St. Norbert's team had a lineup of tall, talented players. Other teams were usually overwhelmed by our team's height, skill, and experience, but not St. Norbert's. We had no advantage over them.

We hoped that one particular game would be our breakthrough. The showdown was against St. Norbert's in the second round on a cold, snowy Saturday night. Rain turned to ice and transformed the roads into ice slicks, then snow fell on top of that mess. It worked to our advantage, however, because one of their star players didn't get there until halftime.

We held our own against them, but toward the end, the score see-sawed back and forth. We had a one-point lead in the final seconds. Their point guard pushed the ball up the floor and launched the ball with only one second on the clock. The buzzer went off while it was midair. Everyone held their breath and watched the ball bounce off the rim and back to the floor. We had won the game!

The place went crazy, and Mark and I, who rode the bench for most of the game, jumped up and down, and we hugged and high-fived anyone we could find. We had not won the tournament yet, but this win felt just as good. It was the highlight of the season, and I daresay it was the highlight of our lives to that point.

The next morning, my family prepared to go to church. I took my time in front of the bathroom mirror, brushing my teeth and combing my hair. I could hear Mom and my older sister, Lynn, talking softly in the living room. I thought I heard Mom laugh. I figured Lynn had just told her a joke or a story. Then Lynn called out to me.

"Joey, come in here," she said flatly.

"All right, I'm almost done," I replied, with no urgency.

"JOEY, GET IN HERE NOW!" she yelled.

I went to the living room and saw my mother's tear-streaked face. I had never seen her so upset. Lynn sat next to her and held one of her hands. Her other arm was around Mom's shoulders.

Dad walked in, phone in hand. He stopped mid-room and looked at the floor. An overwhelming sadness enveloped him, and he was as close to tears as I'd ever seen him.

"Joe, I don't know how to tell you this, but I have some bad news about Mark. He was selling newspapers at his stand this morning, and there was a three-car accident. He was crushed."

My eyebrows shot up, and my jaw dropped. I clearly didn't know what he meant.

Dad continued. "I'm sorry, Joey. Mark is dead."

Time stopped. My stomach muscles twisted, and I collapsed over the back of the chair in front of me. Shock, sadness, and anger hollowed out my insides. Tears came in waves, and I crumpled to the floor.

After a lot of hugs and tears, my parents pulled our family together, and we drove to the school. No one knew exactly what happened to Mark or why. My classmates gathered with their families and the community, and we mourned together. There were few words, but lots of eye contact, tears, and hugs. Mom and Dad let me go to a friend's house to join some other classmates, and for the rest of the day we alternated between deep laughter and crippling tears as everyone shared their favorite memories of our friend, Mark, who we would never see again.

That week, our classes became grief sessions, and our teachers navigated these uncharted waters as best they could. Our English teacher, Ms. Bright, had lost her husband a few years earlier, and she helped us express our grief. She told us to write down all of our feelings, thoughts, and memories. Then, she encouraged us to take our physical frustrations out on a ball in the gym or at outside recess.

The night before the funeral, hordes of family and friends came to pay their respects to Mark. My aunt approached me and said something that impacted my life from that moment on. It was so unexpected, so off base.

"Joe," she said, "just think of the all the things your friend will never have to experience."

Those words broke my heart. "Thank you," I said, but only to be polite.

I walked away. Was she serious? Things he didn't HAVE to experience? That's why this was so hard—because there were so many things Mark wouldn't GET to experience.

From that day forward, Mark's death drove most of my major decisions. The Latin phrase *Carpe Diem*, which means "seize the day," became my life slogan. I wanted to do things in life that I never thought possible, not just because they were options, but because Mark would never get to do them.

At times, I felt like I was living for two people—for Mark and for me—and that I had to have some crazy times to make up for Mark not being around. At other times, I thought that, instead of Mark, I could have been the one to die at age fourteen, and that every moment I had was a moment to experience life, rather than take it for granted.

> I wanted to do things in life that I never thought possible, not just because they were options, but because Mark would never get to do them.

I decided to make my life extraordinary.

CHAPTER 2

Dorm On Fire

In my junior year of college, the healthy self-confidence I had developed was severely tested. As a Resident Assistant (RA) in my dorm, I served in a leadership role, not only for our floor of about fifty underclassmen, but also for the rest of our dorm—almost 1,000 students on nineteen floors. Every RA ran monthly meetings, organized social events, and kept residents up-to-date on campus news. Once or twice a week, each RA had a "duty" night and spent a few hours in the dorm office and did several walking rounds of the building.

It was my duty night, and Michael, a sophomore from Iowa, was my RA partner that evening. He was clean-cut for the most part, but he let his dark hair grow a little shaggy from time to time. He wanted to be a politician and always practiced his people skills with future voters.

We made the ten o'clock rounds of the building and said hello to the students and staff. One of our favorite security people, Annie, worked the front desk. A small, tough, African-American lady, she was shorter than both Michael and me and always had her short hair done to perfection, with a little orange added to the tips.

"How are we doing tonight, Annie?" I asked cheerfully.

"It's too cold for me!" she said with her customary scowl that turned into an immediate smile.

"You need a heavier jacket, like mine," I said and smoothed out the rugged, dark green navy coat I had picked up at a military surplus store.

"Make sure nothing's happening around here, guys," Annie said.

We headed out the door and let in a gust of cold evening air. Annie shivered and scowled some more.

Everything seemed calm, quiet, and safe. When we came back to the front entrance, I glanced at the lounge around the corner from Annie's desk. Through the glass door, I could see that one of the couches had small flames lapping at the seat cushions.

"Mike, look at that," I said.

We looked at the flames and watched them grow. Just twenty feet away, we stood frozen. We were stunned that there was a serious problem that required immediate action. The fire was small, and I dismissed the thought that I could use my heavy jacket to smother the flames. I loved my jacket. It was warmer than anything I'd ever had, and I needed it for the Chicago winter.

"Fire extinguisher," I said with confidence. "We can handle this."

Michael nodded. We hustled toward Annie.

"Mike, go down to the RA office. Maybe there's one in there," I told Michael. "Annie, do you know where there's a fire extinguisher?"

"Nope, what's going on?" she asked.

"There's a small fire in the front lounge," I answered. I opened the door to the stairwell opposite the bank of three elevators, but there was no fire extinguisher on the wall. A moment later, Mike came out.

"I got nothing," he said, and shook his head. "I checked the RA office and the room next door."

I ran back to the lounge, and Michael and Annie were right behind me.

"Oh Lord, look at that!" Annie said.

The small fire had grown into a thick, black haze that filled the glass-enclosed room. Every few seconds, the smoke clouds would shift behind the door to reveal a tall streak of orange and yellow flames. No winter jacket or fire extinguisher would do any good here.

"Call 9-1-1 now," I told Michael.

I reached for the fire alarm, but before my fingers could grasp it, the air was pierced by a siren that blared for the next half hour. Annie had beat me to it.

The smoke darkened, and the heat increased in the small hallway. Flames leapt, and I could smell burning carpet. The smoke escaped the enclosed room through tiny gaps in the window and door frames and pushed into the hallway. We were in trouble.

Annie ran to her desk and notified the rest of the security staff, then Michael emerged from the RA office, holding a fire extinguisher.

"I found one," he said with a mixture of hope and confusion on his face. "What do we do?" he asked.

He expected me to make a decision. I looked at the lounge, looked back at Michael, and at the lounge again. I thought that since the fire was growing so quickly, we could still get in there and stop its spread before the firefighters arrived.

"Let's go in," I said, and tried to mask my doubt. "On three, I'll open the door, and you start spraying."

Michael nodded, gathered his courage, held up the extinguisher, and braced himself to plunge into the mess.

"One, two," I began, then hesitated.

Michael held his ground, eyes on me. "You say the word, Joe."

"All right," I said, and took a deep breath. "When I say three. One."

At that moment, a scene from the movie *Backdraft* flashed through my mind. A fireman had opened the door of a burning building and was blown backward by the inferno, hungry for oxygen. I pictured the door opening and the two of us being blown across the hall by the room's fiery belch. Annie's voice pierced the din of the fire alarm.

"Y'all can't go in there!" she bellowed. "Get back here, and let's get the people out!"

"She's right," I said. "Let's play it safe."

The first wave of students poured out of the stairwells because the fire alarm had disabled the elevators. Recently, the blaring of false alarms had cursed the residents. Sometimes, more than once a night, students had their sleep interrupted by an alarm—an anonymous prank. Fed up with mandatory evacuations, many of them scowled and complained as they came out. But shock and silence prevailed when they saw the legitimate reason for this evacuation. Michael and I told them to keep moving.

Soon enough, the firefighters arrived, and they completely destroyed the lounge in the name of safety. They broke the windows to relieve the pressure in the room and spread water on every surface. Michael and I joined the mass of students who shivered out in the courtyard for over an hour. The firemen took reports and secured the area. Finally, they nailed plywood over the window frames, and everyone returned to their rooms. I thought everything was fine.

Over the next few weeks, however, things were anything but fine. Whenever I walked by the burned-out lounge, the faint odor of charred walls slammed me, and my mind flashed back to the night of the fire. I couldn't control the images. I saw all the confused and scared students standing out in the cold, but most of all, I flashed back to the moment when I froze and couldn't count to three.

It took several weeks to repair the lounge. The damaged furniture and carpets were ripped out, and the burned walls and ceilings were removed. More plywood covered the door and windows. But the one thing they couldn't remove was the smell. On some days, the whole ground floor was well ventilated, and I could walk past the lounge without even thinking about it. On other days, a whiff of smoke greeted me, and that scent instantly brought back my guilt: I had frozen when I was most needed. Michael and I had not charged in the lounge to cool down the room at the first sign of danger. We had hesitated.

I had hesitated.

Everyone had gotten out safe, but if we had acted immediately, we could have prevented so much damage.

My guilt was often triggered by a half-second exposure to the faint smell of smoke. It plunged me into a depression that lasted several hours. I felt worthless and powerless, and tried to convince myself I had done nothing wrong.

My low point came one night after a narrow loss in an intense intramural basketball game. I came back to the dorm full of adrenaline, disappointment, and anger. When I opened the front door, I got slapped with the smell of the fire. I tried to push it down, out, or away somewhere. The night was ruined, and I descended into a funk. I showered and got ready to go out with my girlfriend. We rode a bus downtown, but she knew something wasn't right.

"What's wrong?" Becky asked, as my blank eyes stared straight ahead.

"I don't know," I said.

"Are you mad at me?" she probed.

"No. I'm excited to go out with you tonight," I said, though I sounded like I was trying to convince myself. "We lost our basketball game."

"You don't look so good," she said. "Maybe we should just go back."

Suddenly, tears poured down my face, and I doubled over in the seat. My hands flew to my face, and my whole body shook while the sobs escaped.

"I don't know what's going on," I managed say.

"We need to get you some help," Becky said. She rubbed my back and gave me gentle hugs until I calmed down. At the next stop, we got off and headed back to campus.

With Becky's encouragement and a suggestion from my supervisor, I made an appointment with the campus counseling center. I didn't want to go because I thought that only severely traumatized or depressed people should get that kind of help. I was fine overall, except for this little hiccup. Over the next few weeks, I talked to a professional listener for the first time.

In our first few sessions, I talked about life and my recent experience with the fire. My counselor was a calm, soft-spoken, red-haired woman in her mid-twenties, who was working to get the hours she needed for her certification. I didn't mind her lack of full credentials. She seemed to know what she was doing.

During our third session, she asked deeper questions. She had peeled off the levels of my consciousness like the skin of an onion, and now she was close to the core. We hoped to find answers.

"Close your eyes, and picture yourself walking down a hallway. Can you do that?" she asked.

"Sure," I said, as I lay on a comfortable couch.

"Pick a door and walk through it," she said.

"Okay."

"Why do you feel bad?" she asked.

"I let people down."

"How?"

"I wasn't strong. I didn't do the right thing," I said.

"There's another door in that room. Go through it," she said.

"Okay, I'm in the next room."

"Why do you have to do the right thing?" she asked.

"Because I'm Joe. People know me. They know I'm a good person. I do my best. I have to do the right thing?" It was a statement, but I posed it as a question. I was throwing out possible answers and looking for her approval.

"Why?" she asked with a little more urgency.

"I don't want other people to hate me," I answered with a slightly defensive tone. Tears pressed against my closed eyes. My own words confused me.

"In this room, there's one more door. It might be locked. You have to open it," she said.

Tears ran down the sides of my head, back toward my ears. "I'm opening the door," I told her. I had no clue where this was going.

"Now look around. Why does Joe have to do the right thing? Why does Joe have to impress people? What's behind that door?" she asked.

"Because. . ." I started.

I barely managed to get the words out. "Because I don't want to hate myself."

I sobbed for a long time. She offered me tissues and assured me that it was okay to let it all out. With no tears left, I breathed easy again. We ended our session there, and a heavy weight had lifted.

I don't want to hate myself.

I had always thought my actions were driven by a desire to please others, but it turned out that I wanted to avoid negative feelings about myself. Once I saw what drove my thoughts and actions, I took back control of my emotions. I met with my counselor for several more sessions, and we explored how and why I had discovered that truth. In our last session, we agreed that I had reached a level of confidence and peace.

> Once I saw what drove my thoughts and actions, I took back control of my emotions.

"How do you feel?" she asked me.

"I feel better than I have in weeks," I said with relief.

"We've reached a good point. It's up to you whether you want to come back."

"I think I'm good for now. Thank you so much for everything. This experience taught me a lot."

My entire outlook had changed. I used to help others to avoid feeling bad about myself. The counseling sessions taught me to embrace the person that I am, warts and all, which gave me the confidence I needed to pursue the life I wanted to live.

CHAPTER 3

Odd Jobs

"Dad, what time do you get up to go to work?" I was only seven, and I asked my dad a lot of questions.

"Six thirty," he said.

"Why?"

"So I can beat traffic."

"What time do you get off work?"

"Three thirty."

"Why?"

"So I can beat traffic."

"What do you do?"

"I'm a Systems Analyst at the Postal Data Center."

That was too many big words for my young brain. "So what do you *do*?" I repeated.

"I work on computers at the post office."

"Do you like it?"

"It's fine. I like to get home, so I can be with you and your brother and sisters," said Dad, with a pat on my head.

"But do you really like being at work?"

"Not really, but I have to go."

"Why?"

"So we can live in our house, drive our cars, and have all the stuff we have."

My dad's reason for working at a job that he didn't love is familiar to a lot of working people. He needed to earn money, and his hours allowed him to be home in the afternoon to be with his kids. Dad lived to be with us. He coached us in basketball, baseball, and softball, which were sports that he had excelled in as a youth. He also coached or assisted with soccer, which he was not that good at, but we didn't know that. When I was in the fifth grade, a group of kids gathered, and we needed one more player, so our teams would be even for a scrimmage.

"Joe's Dad can play with us," one of my teammates suggested.

"Sure! Dad, be on my team!" I said.

"I'm not really dressed for it," Dad said, and tried to ease away.

"Who cares? We need you," I said with finality.

After the scrimmage started, I saw why Dad had hesitated. Someone passed him the ball, and he headed toward the goal while a few defenders chased him.

"Dad, pass! I'm wide open," I shouted with my hands up, right in front of the goal.

He hustled and tried to maneuver his legs to kick the ball to me. The other team closed in. He couldn't make the pass and lost the ball.

"Sorry, Joey, I just couldn't get it to you," said Dad.

I paused. For the first time, I realized that Dad wasn't good at everything. I had never consciously thought that Dad was good at *everything*, but it never occurred to me that there might be something he couldn't do. I was confused at first, then felt a little disappointed, but overall, I was happy that Dad wanted to be with me, regardless of his soccer skills.

As a dad myself, I now see how every dad is a hero to his boy. And that's why I was confused by Dad's perspective about work. It didn't seem to fit with the rest of him. He was the most positive, confident, good-spirited guy you could meet. But he hated work, and I couldn't wrap my mind around doing something you didn't like.

> I had never consciously thought that Dad was good at *everything*, but it never occurred to me that there might be something he couldn't do.

I continued to ask questions, and when I was around eleven or twelve years old, I wanted to know more about what Dad did at work.

"How long have you been working on computers?" I asked.

"Oh, about ten years," he said with a sigh.

"Will you ever," I hesitated, "move up or get promoted?"

"I probably could if I wanted to," he said.

"So why don't you? Wouldn't that mean making more money?" I asked.

"I don't really want to."

"Why not?" I wondered.

"Well, the guys that move up tend to be brown-nosers," Dad said, which I sort of understood at that age. "I'm just not that kind of guy."

I admired that Dad stayed true to himself, but still questioned why he never wanted to improve his situation.

"Plus," he added, "I'm in a union, which is nice and stable. That's important because Mom and I have the four of you to take care of. I want to keep things like they are."

I didn't know what a union was, but Dad had a reason for his position, and I accepted it. He took good care of his family.

Dad's career gave me a strong example of a solid work ethic with a primary focus on providing for the family. But the most important thing I learned from his work experience was what I didn't want. Our parents had always encouraged us to do our best, to pursue the highest honors, and to gain the recognition. They programmed us to seek advancement, to go higher and further. Yet, it seemed like had Dad settled in his own career. He was showing me that being an adult meant that you had to provide for your family every day, suck it up, and report to a job that you didn't like. Giving eight hours a day to a job you didn't like was a small price to pay to support the family you loved.

Except.

That meant spending a lot of time doing things you didn't like— or that you even hated. I had heard that the average life span is about seventy-five years and that we spend a third of it sleeping. Another third is spent at work, which doesn't leave a whole lot. I wondered why my dad, who in general seemed to love his life, spent so much time and effort doing something he didn't enjoy.

With all my heart, I wanted to find something I loved to do. My reason was simple: If you could do something you loved, wouldn't that make one-third of your life that much more amazing?

My family was far from rich, did not go on fancy vacations, have a pool, or live in a mansion. But my parents saw to it that we didn't lack for the essentials, and they taught us to work for what we really wanted.

Dad mandated that we get part-time jobs in high school and college to help pay for living expenses and college tuition. It didn't matter what we did, as long as we earned something.

For two summers, I worked part-time for a family friend who owned a landscaping business. He picked me up at six o'clock every morning, and we cut grass for the next ten hours. Despite the oppressive heat of the St. Louis summers, our standard work clothes were boots, long pants, hats, earplugs, and safety glasses. As a bonus, I got to wear the dirt packed under my fingernails for the first few weeks of school. Whenever we crossed paths in later years, I told my old boss how he taught me to have a good work ethic. I don't tell him that he also taught me to avoid outdoor employment.

For two other summers, I had office jobs. I learned that there were companies that match you with temporary positions, and they offered decent pay. I ended up in a nondescript office, where a bunch of adults in cubicles ran around, made a lot of copies, and sometimes had me make copies for them. The water cooler conversations reminded me that I was miserable.

"Did you get caught in that traffic jam this morning?" asked one of the older workers.

"Yeah, that construction is a killer," I replied with little interest.

"Good to be inside in weather like this. It's summers like these I don't mind working in a cool, comfortable cubicle."

"Hmm."

"I can't wait till five o'clock, got some big plans tonight. How about you?" he asked.

"I don't know, haven't thought about it," I said.

"Well, it's only Monday. Can't get too crazy, gotta be back here at eight!" he chuckled.

"Don't remind me," I said.

"Don't worry, Joe, only four days till the weekend!"

Here I was, a college kid on summer vacation with an early morning drive to a cubicle. I looked forward to the end of every day and lived to finish the week on Friday. I didn't learn much, and definitely did not enjoy myself.

One day I joined some other college-age cohorts for lunch, and when we passed in front of the building, I caught my reflection in the glass. I saw a guy who wore a red, short-sleeve polo shirt tucked into pleated khaki pants and scuffed dress shoes from the thrift store. His gait looked familiar, and his arms swung lazily back and forth. I couldn't yet see the bald head or middle-age paunch, but they seemed to be a foregone conclusion. It was a younger version of Dad that stared back at me, and I never wanted to see that again.

The next summer I wanted to get a job that meant something, but I waited too long to look for it. Pretty soon I was back on the phone with a temp service.

"We only have two openings right now, but you won't want the second one," the operator said.

"What is it?" I asked.

"The first one is an office job. The second one is at Six Flags."

"Tell me about the Six Flags job," I said.

"It's only for three weeks, and it's in the games department," the operator said.

"You mean like working the game booths?" I asked.

"I don't know, it just says games," she said.

"I'll take it."

I worked in a warehouse just outside of the Batman ride, where we caught and enticed people to spend money to play games like skeeball, bottle-toss, and Crusher, the classic game where players use a hammer to bang the heads of plastic rodents that spastically pop up. The Crusher operator had a microphone and announced all the activity inside the warehouse.

The first morning I was at the bottle-toss game, which required zero brain activity from me or the players. For a dollar or two, they threw beanbags at a pyramid of bottles for cheap prizes. A nice girl with limited wit or vocal ability was on the Crusher microphone. I paid little attention to her uninspired words before lunch, but the supervisor asked me if I wanted a shot in the afternoon. Microphone work? It took me half a second to say "yes."

I had a blast with that microphone. I crushed the Crusher!

"Come play the Crusher!"

"Win prizes at the Crusher!"

"Tell your Mom to bring you to the Crusher!" I said and looked into each kid's eyes as their Moms dragged them in the other direction. I did impressions, changed my voice, got excited, and loved it. Within an hour, the supervisor's boss approached.

"I want to give you a full-time job here for the rest of the summer," he said.

Flattered, I asked, "At what pay?"

He told me I would make what everyone else made, which was hardly anything.

"I'll only be here for three weeks," I said. "Let's see what happens, and I'll let you know if I change my mind."

Six Flags, like so many other theme parks, attracts its workers with the glamour of a job at a fancy, famous location. The thrill that underpaid teen workers get outweighs their lack of compensation. I knew I was capable of bigger and better things. I just didn't have a clue what those things were yet.

> I knew I was capable of bigger and better things. I just didn't have a clue what those things were yet.

When I was driving home, I saw a sign on a lightpost that advertised work for students at a high rate of pay. I wrote the number down and called for an interview, with zero knowledge of anything about the job. I showed up at their nondescript office building and sat in a conference room with a bunch of other students.

The purpose of this group interview wasn't obvious right away, but when the manager pulled out a set of kitchen knives, I felt a lightning strike of excitement. I remembered talking to a friend about options for summer jobs awhile back. He had said, "You could be like Chris over there who sold knives and made thousands of dollars every summer."

"That's not real," I said and dismissed the thought. It couldn't possibly be true.

Now this manager from Cutco showed us how we could do it ourselves. I sold knives that summer, and my perspective about a lot of things changed. During my training, the manager talked a lot about opportunity. I was very skeptical, and refused to believe this system could work. In fact, I decided to prove that it wouldn't and determined to do everything he said, just to prove the operation was a total sham.

I followed his instructions to the tee and never came close to proving him wrong.

The sales part didn't come easy, but it challenged me to constantly learn, implement, and interact with people, which energized me like no other job before. Very few of us made much money in the beginning, including me. At one point, my very by-the-book Dad and nervous Mom sat down with me to do the math.

"Why keep pursuing sales where you have no guaranteed income, when you could work x number of hours and be assured x amount of dollars?" Dad asked with a firm tone. He was a not a salesman.

"I'm not thrilled about you being in sales," Mom said. "Your Grandpa sold insurance, and it was not an easy life."

"Just let me try this," I insisted. To their credit, they let me find my way.

As it turned out, I had a knack for sales. That summer, while I probably made just as much or even a bit less money than I had in previous summers, I built a business. The income I generated was up to me, and I did what was required to succeed. I put in serious phone time and called people and set up appointments. I planned my workdays, drove to people's homes, gave demonstrations, and filled out and submitted order forms. I also attended three or four meetings a week to learn how to do it better. The office Top Ten list showed the ladder I could climb, and it inspired me to give my maximum effort. I loved the fact that I didn't know anyone else who had this job. I became successful in something I'd discovered on my own, and I loved it!

In addition, I realized that I could have a career that didn't look like Dad's. Yes, there was an office that the managers used, but my workplace was in my customers' homes or in my own basement with the phone. I could be mobile at work instead of being parked in a cubicle all day.

Constant rejection is part of every sales job—both on the phone and in person. But I also had the disapproval of my family to contend with, and not just from my parents. I drove almost an hour to my aunt's farm one day because she agreed to see a presentation about the knives. My grandma, the widow of my insurance salesman grandfather, also joined us. When I finished my presentation, I asked if they wanted to buy anything.

"I think you need to find another line of work, Joey," my aunt said.

"I don't like it, but I'll buy one knife," said my grandma.

Those words stung, but I drove away determined that I would succeed, no matter what. By the end of that summer, I knew I had made headway, even with my parents.

"This is your last week. How are sales going?" my mom asked.

"I'm stressed," I said. "I'm right at the brink of winning this sales contest, but I need one more sale and don't know where I'll get it."

Mom was quiet for a minute, then said, "There is one knife I need. I'll be your customer."

I was well on my way to my life of unconventional employment.

CHAPTER 4

The Stand-Up Comedian in a Wolf Suit

Like most college kids, I never had a lot of money, but that didn't stop me from having fun. Being short of cash forced me to examine job opportunities I might not have considered. One ad described a marketing study where I could be paid forty dollars or more to listen to a product description for an hour. That worked for me, so I looked for and found other things like that.

My freshman year, I wanted to be a RA for my dorm, so I applied for the job. My reasons were both personal and financial. The RAs received countless hours of training on people skills, and I liked that idea. We also got to live in the dorms for free, which I loved because I didn't have to buy groceries or cook meals. In short, the job included free room and board.

I took advantage of such opportunities that were available to everyone, but few pursued. Posters in our classrooms and hallways offered treasures and priceless experiences that most students didn't even glance at. I read them all. One flyer in particular stood out. The large print at the top said *Have you ever wanted to be a comedian?*

> Posters in our classrooms and hallways offered treasures and priceless experiences that most students didn't even glance at. I read them all.

I told my roommate about it. "Dude, I'm gonna be a stand-up comedian!"

"What are you talking about?" he asked.

"There's a contest in two weeks, and I signed up," I said. "The top three get cash prizes."

"What are you gonna say?" he asked.

"I don't know yet, but I'll think of something."

"You should do an impression, you're great at those. Do an impression of the school president," he suggested.

"Father Piderit?" I wasn't so sure about impersonating the President of Loyola University.

"Totally. You're not bald, but you can do his girly, old-man voice and talk about 'THREE POINTS' like he always does in his speeches," he said.

"You think so? Everybody would definitely know that one," I said.

I wrote a short routine that included an impression of our quirky school president, plus some jokes about the "L" trains in Chicago. Although it was not a landmark success, I held my own on stage. But my roommate missed it! He was off campus with some friends and didn't make it back in time, but we caught up the next morning.

"Good morning!" he yelled. He barged into our room and plopped onto his bed. "Tell me about your comedy routine!"

I rubbed my eyes, stretched my arms, and smiled. "It was awesome," I declared.

"Sweet! How did the Piderit impression go?"

"Not bad. People recognized it and laughed. It needs some work," I said.

"Did you do the "L" train jokes?" he said.

"Eh, I might have to change those up a bit. But it was all good. People clapped for me."

"So what did you win?"

"Nothing. I came in fourth, so no cash for me. But no worries, man. At least I got on stage."

"You're an official comedian!" he laughed.

Now I had something new to love—being on stage and in front of people.

And then there was another flyer. This time it was for the school mascot and spirit team tryouts. I knew I didn't want to be a cheerleader, but I was intrigued with the idea of being a mascot. I showed up at the gym and found a woman who looked official.

"Are you in charge?" I asked.

"Yes, how can I help you?" she said, eyes locked on her clipboard.

"I saw cheerleaders on that side of the gym, but no one is over here. Is this the mascot tryouts?"

She looked up. "You want to be the mascot?" she said.

"Uh, sure," I answered.

"Great. Be here next Tuesday. You can be the mascot."

"That's it?" I asked.

"See you next Tuesday," she said with a trace of a courtesy smile.

On Tuesday I was given a wolf costume. Gray fur covered the full body suit, which zipped up in the back. I slipped my feet, shoes on, into oversized wolf paws, and my hands fit into gloves covered in the same gray fur. The head for Lou the Wolf had a fantastic wolf face that would have made Walt Disney cringe. The nose was perched at the end of a long wolf mouth and that bared its stuffed, pointed teeth. Cartoon eyes were painted over thin black screens that allowed me to see out, but never straight ahead.

When I put it on, I realized that the job held little glamour. The head piece, heavy and stuffed, felt warm at first, but heated up to sauna status fast. I was sweating in seconds. On top of the heat, my own sweat activated the dormant sweat and its odor from several years of previous mascot men. The stench was easy to ignore because my nose got used to it after a little while, but there was no escape from the heat. I soaked through several t-shirts in one game alone.

One of my favorite moves as the mascot was to find a beautiful girl from my own dorm. I'd sit next to her, flirt, put my arm around her, and ham it up. She had no idea who was inside the suit, and all my friends who sat nearby laughed and loved it. When I saw the girl in the dorm later, I'd ask her about the mascot.

"The mascot sat by you today—how about that?" I said.

"He was crazy! I don't know what he was doing!" she responded.

My three years as the school mascot brought some unexpected benefits. I had always wanted to go to every game, and now I could, although I couldn't just sit and watch it like a normal person. In fact, my job wasn't to watch the game, but to entertain the people in the seats.

Even as a Division I program, our school had never been known for basketball after we'd won the National Championship in the 1960s. Mediocre team and small arena aside, I now had the opportunity to be in front of big crowds. I could act silly with no social consequences. Other than the honor of being recognized at Senior Day and getting an invitation to the sports banquet, I never received any compensation for being the school mascot. But I found another unique experience the world offered—and it makes a great story.

I had laid a foundation for big things to come.

CHAPTER 5

Money Matters

St. Louis University High School, an all-boys private college prep school, both expanded my horizons and offered lasting lessons in humility. For the first time, I met people from different parts of St. Louis, and everyone came from different backgrounds.

Students from less privileged families could work off a portion of their tuition in a program called Work Grant. We worked for a grant, which meant we spent afternoons, Saturdays, and summer weeks at school. We painted walls, cleaned out garages, landscaped, and pretty much did anything we could to pass the time on those unenjoyable shifts.

My confidence from my soccer success in earlier grades propelled me to some quick victories in high school. Because our school had a thousand students, we had enough boys to form three teams for every sport: varsity for juniors and seniors, junior varsity for sophomores, and the freshman team. We were a soccer powerhouse, and a few weeks before school started, I tried out for the freshman team.

From the first day, I didn't fit in. My speed matched anybody out there, and my skills were at least above average, but the guys who were much better than me had two big advantages. Most of them had played soccer year-round for their school, as well as in indoor leagues and on select teams. Lots of them already knew each other.

They also dressed the part. Expensive, fancy soccer shorts matched their shiny shirts from soccer camp, a tournament, or a team. They carried their pricey Adidas shoes in fancy soccer bags with special pockets for expensive state-of-the-art shin guards.

As for me, I could hide my humble, tiny shin guards under my knee-high soccer socks, and I could juggle the handful of decent soccer shorts

I'd gotten for Christmas presents or at clearance sales. But I could not hide my shoes.

"Where'd you get those shoes?" one guy asked me.

His hair was perfectly gelled. His shorts looked like they came from a European soccer league. His shirt boasted first place in some state tournament with a big local soccer club. His hundred-dollar shoes gleamed and showed a few scuff marks, but the name and logo on the side made him fit right in with the other divas on the field. He eyed my humble pair of cleats—a worn pair of soccer spikes, at least two years old, that hung on for dear life.

"I don't remember," I lied. I didn't want to tell him the name of the department store that was near our house.

"Huh," he said. "I've never seen those before."

I was not surprised that I made the first cut, but I held no illusion about making the team. The other guys had the advantage of a privileged background and deeper experience. Still, soccer was my favorite sport, and I had been successful before. I knew I could play, and I didn't care what my clothes, shoes, or hair looked like while playing.

Incredibly, I found my name was on the final team list! As it turned out, the coaches chose more players than they had originally planned. It felt like I stuck out—along with three other guys—as the bottom rungs on the ladder, but that didn't matter. I had made my first high school sports team!

That thrill faded fast, and the torturous season stretched on forever. Nothing clicked between my teammates and me. I was smaller and less experienced, but more than that, my heart wasn't in it. The coach and my parents encouraged me to stick it out when I wanted to quit. The end of that season was a relief, and I turned my attention to basketball tryouts.

Just like soccer, dozens of guys came out for the team. And just like soccer, my speed matched up with anyone, but not necessarily my size or skill. I had even less hope to make this team. Still, I gave it my all.

The first cuts were posted on the bulletin board outside the cafeteria. Several people said, "Congratulations," as they walked by. I thought they were joking. Then I read the list. My name was one of the few included amongst the taller guys who were built to play basketball.

Our class had a handful of tall, talented guards. Unfortunately, the final list posted a few days later did not include my name.

I was disappointed, but I understood. I wasn't good enough for that level of competition. That experience forced me to learn how to deal with rejection. I tried out for and got cut from every other sport at school, including volleyball, baseball, sophomore soccer, and every year in basketball.

I am cheap to the core and won't deny it. I'm sure my parents had a lot to do with it. Of course, I could object to the term "cheap," and claim I'm simply being "frugal," but it's not true. I always look for ways to cut corners to save money.

When we were kids, Dad gave us each a quarter every Sunday for allowance. One week, I thought Dad put out an extra quarter by accident, so I pocketed it. When my older sister came out to look for hers, it wasn't there. The tension was high as my parents looked on and around the table for her quarter. They were not going to give her another one. I managed to slip the quarter back on the table without any commotion. That experience stuck with me, and I learned that if I wanted money, I had to earn it.

We didn't have a lot of money, and we always focused on getting the most value from every dollar. We always went to Busch Stadium, home of our beloved baseball Cardinals, fully stocked. There were six of us, and we brought our big thermos of Kool-Aid and several brown bags full of sandwiches and snacks. Concession stand food was too expensive, so we had to pass on that.

Mom did most of her grocery shopping at Aldi, which only accepts cash and doesn't even take coupons. I didn't know it then, but she had to take her own grocery bags, load her own groceries, and deposit a quarter just to use a shopping cart. You can be sure that we always got that quarter back. For these inconveniences, Aldi gave its customers the lowest prices in town. But then again, they didn't sell name-brand stuff, and we always got a kick out of the generic soda and cereal that were obvious

> The Aldi experience showed how we Fingerhuts operated: Go without the frills and save your money.

ripoffs of the real thing: Dr. Schnee instead of Dr. Pepper, Fruit Rounds instead of Fruit Loops, and so on. The Aldi experience showed how we Fingerhuts operated: Go without the frills and save your money.

Instead of a piggy bank, I saved my money in an old plastic butter container with a slit in the lid. Every coin I found went in there. Occasionally, I emptied it out on my bed and stacked the handful of one-dollar bills next to the piles of four quarters, next to the piles of ten dimes, and on down the line, until everything was counted. One time, I had over sixty-three dollars. I looked at that pile on my bed and felt like I was rich. I didn't ever want it to shrink.

Our family policy was that if we wanted to buy something, we had to pay for half of it ourselves—a good lesson in delayed gratification. Because of that rule, I gave up hope of getting several things I wanted, including a battery powered Lego train. I thought I wanted it, but when I figured out how much it would cost me, the train lost a lot of appeal. I could live without it.

I learned to leverage our parents' policy in my favor, and eventually my taste in shoes matured from simple, inexpensive Chuck Taylors to the new style of basketball shoes I called Puffy Shoes. They were outrageously expensive, and my lust for them was powered by my admiration of Michael Jordan. I had to have these shoes and, why not? I only had to pay half. But my parents didn't buy it. Right there, they changed the policy and said they'd only pay up to $30 for shoes. We would have to take care of the rest. I still have a healthy fascination with shoes, but the discipline my parents instilled in me prevents me from overspending.

I didn't care so much about my hair and often went too long between haircuts because I didn't want to pay someone to cut it. I hung on to clothes for too long, and stocked up on free t-shirts like they were sewn with golden thread. I avoided sports that required a lot of equipment or a specific field time, like football and hockey. When I was in college, I once shopped for clothes at a store called Structure, and when they had an end-of-season clearance sale, I thought I had won the lottery. Multiple shirts, pants, and a winter coat later, I marked my mental calendar to remember to shop at the end of the season, whether I needed clothes or not.

At Cutco, most of my co-workers and some of the managers were also students in their late teens or early twenties. A major focus of the company, besides teaching us how to sell knives, was an emphasis on our personal and financial education.

Twice a summer, my manager chartered a bus with a few dozen sales reps, and he took us to Dallas, where we joined several hundred reps for a few days' worth of educational seminars and motivational rallies. At the first conference, one of the young, successful managers gave a presentation about how to make, keep, and save money.

"The most important thing you have on your side is *time*," he said.

He had a big pad of paper attached to an easel, and he told us about the "Rule of 72."

"Einstein said, 'The most powerful force in the universe is compound interest.' Let me illustrate it for you."

He grabbed a marker and wrote "$1,000."

"Let's say you have one thousand dollars," he said. "If you invest that money somewhere that grows by 10% every year, compound interest will make it grow."

He listed a few more numbers, and explained, "The bottom line is: if you put away just a little money on a regular basis, it will double on its own over time. In this example, $1,000 becomes $2,000 in about seven years."

I sat in silence, scribbled some notes, and tried to comprehend it all. His message stuck: You can double an amount of money in seven years if you save it in the right place. That made sense.

"What's next?" he continued. "Why is this a big deal? Well, let's say you are age twenty when you invest that first $1,000. Look at the total every seven years." He flipped another page.

> You can double an amount of money in seven years if you save it in the right place.

Age 20:	$ 1,000
Age 27:	$ 2,000
Age 34:	$ 4,000
Age 41:	$ 8,000
Age 48:	$ 16,000
Age 55:	$ 32,000
Age 62:	$ 64,000

The guy next to leaned over and whispered, "So you put away money, and it doubles," he said. "Over time, it becomes bigger. So what?"

As if reading his mind, the speaker said, "Here's where it gets interesting. What if we get aggressive, and instead of investing only $1,000, we make it $10,000? So you add a zero to everything."

He flipped to another page.

Age 20: $ 10,000
Age 27: $ 20,000
Age 34: $ 40,000
Age 41: $ 80,000
Age 48: $ 160,000
Age 55: $ 320,000
Age 62: $ 640,000

My eyebrows shot up when I saw that last number. Then he dropped the bomb.

"Here's the best part. Let's say this is you. You managed to put together $10,000 at age twenty and forgot about it. Without lifting a finger, we can see what how it grows. What if you wait a few more years before you touch it?"

He flipped to the last page.

START: Age 20: $ 10,000
END: Age 69: $1,280,000

"At age 69, you will have $1.2 million dollars," he concluded.

The room went nuts! Everybody clapped and screamed, and I gave the guy next to me a high five.

"You all have this opportunity," he said. "Start now. Use time to your advantage. Best of luck."

From then on, funding my retirement through my own savings was at the top of my list. Every time I ordered water at a restaurant instead of paying for a soda, packed my own lunch instead of buying something, or chose to buy a used car instead of a new one, I had retirement on my mind.

I had this goal but never stopped to think about why I needed a million dollars or what I would do with it. But I took action anyway. Those answers would come later.

I didn't have $10,000, but when we returned home from that conference, I moved forward. My boss referred me to his financial planner. I set up an appointment, and soon made my first investment. I put a few hundred dollars into a retirement account, and I felt very important.

My relationship with money swung between feelings of scarcity and feelings of abundance. We were raised in an atmosphere of scarcity. As I grew older, on some days I feared the future and on other days, it seemed like money rained from the clouds. No matter what the situation, the need for money is real, and it can create stress. My attitude about money is somewhat schizophrenic. I know I need it, but because I don't care deeply about it, I have to force myself to focus on it. I've never bought a new car and really don't intend to, since you lose nearly 20 percent when you drive it off the lot. If you pay top dollar for a vacation, you probably paid someone else probably to plan it for you, and while that sounds like fun, you can save a lot of money and appreciate the trip more if you plan it yourself.

If money were the most important thing to me, instead of doing what I love, I would have pursued a career with the highest earning potential. Perhaps I would have gone with an early startup company or some other endeavor that had the potential of a huge payout. But I would have missed the crazy and fun path I've been on since college graduation.

Instead, I chose work that had the highest happiness potential. It took a while to build momentum and get established in my career as an entertainer, and I've never had a huge surplus of money. So I've had to manage my money with careful attention.

> Instead, I chose work that had the highest happiness potential.

My dream was to have a career as an entertainer and a speaker. In the early years, I constantly called prospective clients and tried to hustle business, but as time went on I made fewer calls, and more people reached out to me because I'd become known for the various skills I developed. I did what I loved, and the money followed.

CHAPTER 6

Family Matters

My parents always supported my goals and decisions, but every once in a while their true feelings broke through. My hard work in high school resulted in not quite great, but good grades, and Mom and Dad pledged their support for whatever college I chose to attend.

"As long as the cost of school is in the ballpark of what we can find for you around St. Louis, you can go wherever you want," Dad said.

We'd taken a few road trips to visit colleges, and I got extra input from friends and family. I considered all this information, as well as my guidance counselor's input. As my senior year continued, my parents encouraged me to make a decision. I decided to share it with the whole family at dinner.

I sat next to my younger sister, Katie, and across from my brother, Mark. Mom claimed one end of the table and Dad the other. Our sister, Lynn, lived at college, so there was an empty chair next to Dad. We passed the meat loaf and scooped out helpings of mashed potatoes. I waited for a pause in the conversation before jumping in.

"I think I want to go to Loyola University Chicago," I said. I looked at Mom first, then at Dad.

She took about a half-second to react.

"You're gonna have to put up with that cold wind coming off that lake!" she said sharply, then stabbed a piece of meat loaf and stuffed it in her mouth. I'd heard that tone before. It was the same one she used when she scolded me as a boy.

I looked at the frown on her face, then to the other end where Dad stared down at his food. I didn't know what to think.

"Why is that your decision?" Dad asked.

"I have only lived in St. Louis," I said. "I want to experience life in a bigger city."

Silverware scraped on plates, and no one said a word.

"I thought you said I could go wherever I wanted," I said softly to Mom.

"I guess we were hoping you would pick somewhere closer," she said.

"At least I'm not going to Texas," I said. We had visited a few schools near Dallas. I'd been impressed with several of the schools, but I didn't want to be that far away.

"Well, at least you've made a decision," Mom said. I could tell that she wasn't thrilled.

The funny thing is that this is what my parents had taught me to do—to think for myself—and their support throughout my life had given me the confidence to make this decision. Even though it wasn't their preference, I knew that whatever decision I made, it had to be right for me. Where to go to college was the first major decision I had made, and being firm about that choice helped me make other decisions later.

> Instead of losing touch with my family, going away to college had a positive effect on my relationships with my younger brother and sister, Mark and Katie.

Instead of losing touch with my family, going away to college had a positive effect on my relationships with my younger brother and sister, Mark and Katie. As the second of four, I was both a younger brother and an older brother. My older sister, Lynn, got a lot of attention as a tall, smart, and athletic girl. Her achievements motivated me, and I always pushed to match her good grades and athletic accomplishments. I also wanted to be as tall as she was.

We had our share of arguments and fights as kids, and in high school, Lynn did some positive 'big-sister' things like taking me along with her friends for nights out. But overall, she seemed to enjoy her independence and didn't open up often or let any of us get to know her very well.

I always wanted more from Lynn. This gap in our relationship drove me to nurture the bond with Mark and Katie. Even though it seemed like our childhood was louder, more contentious, and more physical than it should have been, in retrospect it looked normal. Siblings, after all, fight; it's in the job description.

When I came home from my first semester of college, I sat down in private with my brother Mark first, and then Katie.

"I'm your older brother, but I also want to be friends with you," I told them. "I want to get to know you and be open about my life, in case my experiences can help you with yours."

That first conversation was pretty awkward. They were younger, less mature, and not really sure what I meant. But it started us on the path of shared experiences and close friendships.

Mark and Katie each came up to Chicago to visit me at Loyola, and I gave them both the full experience. I was open about everything I had done, so they could see what their life may be like in a few years—and be excited about it. Since I was away from home, I didn't know a lot about their day-to-day lives, but the bond I had wanted to create was well established by the time my college years were over.

During both high school and college I learned a valuable lesson: Friendships have an ebb and flow similar to the ocean tides. Sometimes I'd feel as close as brothers with someone, but then something as simple as a change in our schedules could turn us into acquaintances in a matter of weeks. The foundation of our friendship could certainly last, but a deep friendship demands close proximity at some point. Life doesn't always make that possible.

After a few months as RAs, my friend—another Katie—and I knew each other pretty well. She often called me to get a "guy's perspective" on a boy problem, and she gave valuable input when I needed a "girl's perspective."

"My Dad once told me," she said, "that you'll have maybe six or seven great friends in your life."

"I totally disagree with that," I immediately said.

"Well think about it. He's right."

"No, he's not. I can think of twenty friends off the top of my head."

"Then tell me. Who are your great friends?"

"Easy." I named a bunch of people: three from high school, two from grade school, and several from college. But then I realized that we probably wouldn't stay in touch forever. I thought about the decades that would follow our college years.

"Wow. I think I see how your dad could be right," I said. "Let's try to be one of the six or seven to each other."

"You got it," she answered.

With graduation ahead, a major stage in my life would end soon, and I began to feel anxious about the future. I would no longer be a student, given specific instructions from a set of teachers. The safety net of my parents had already diminished over my college years, but after graduation, that net would be all but gone. There was a big question mark about how I would go forward.

I met with the hall director of my dorm, and she listened to my dark impression of the post-college years. She asked me what my specific fears were.

"Finding a job, a good partner, starting a family, just general responsibility," I told her.

"You're gonna love your 20s," she said. "You can do whatever you want. Even if you make a bad decision, you're the one who made it. It's your life, and you get to choose how to live it."

That comment completely changed my thinking, and I got more excited about graduation. I realized I was ready to take the next step, and I could do so with all the enthusiasm and joy that life had delivered thus far.

Chapter 7

Dad Said "No" to Europe

The summer before my senior year, it hit me that I had never been outside the United States. After graduation, it would be jobs, bills, and the big bore of adulthood, so I decided to do whatever it took to get out of the country and have some crazy experiences before 'the rest of my life' began. Of course, I wanted to talk to my dad about it.

The warm, summer air had cooled as Dad and I headed to the backyard. We sat down at the old, green picnic table for a Saturday evening talk. The benches and table looked weak, but the old wood, weathered and cracked, rested on a robust steel frame. This table had hosted more than a few important talks between us that summer, but this night became the most memorable. Tonight was the night I would tell Dad my grand plan. I pictured him patting me on the back and saying, "Let's find a way to make this happen."

"I want to study in Europe," I began. "My plan is to take an extra semester and study at Loyola's campus in Rome."

He said nothing, so I continued.

"I'm gonna get through this next year, finish up all my math classes for my major, then do an extra semester in Europe," I said. "I know it will cost extra money in student loans and will mean extra time in school, but I've done the research and talked to a lot of people about it. I really want to do this."

Dad concentrated and absorbed every point. He neither smiled nor frowned. He gave a short sigh before destroying my dreams.

"That's not gonna happen," he said. Flat tone.

"What?" I asked. "Why?"

Then he took his verbal machine gun and ripped apart my aspirations.

"It's too expensive. Where are you gonna stay? How are you gonna get around? What are you going to eat? Where are you going to eat? Do they speak English? Is it safe? Do they like Americans? What about eating? Where are you gonna eat?"

His questions popped up like those stupid rodents in Crusher. He didn't even give me time to whack them.

"May I remind you that after this year," he continued, "you will get no help from Mom and me? Four years for college, and that's it. You say you'll take on extra debt, but do you have any idea how much one semester costs?"

I sat silent.

"Besides, it's dangerous over there," Dad said. "How do you know you're not going to end up in a bad situation?"

I looked away, feeling worse with every second.

"You don't even know if they speak English or if they like Americans."

He paused, determined to voice every ounce of his discouragment.

"And when you get back, everyone that graduated will have taken all the jobs."

I fought back tears.

"It's your dream, and I hope it comes true," Dad said, and then dropped the hammer. "But it's a pipe dream. It's not gonna happen."

Tears tumbled through my hands and down my cheeks. They were not, however, tears of defeat. I was deeply sad that one of the most important people in my life would not be my ally on this journey. I solidified my determination and knew I would make it happen.

Fine, I thought defiantly. *If I can't study in Europe, I'm going to Europe without studying.*

I just had to figure out how.

Before I traveled around Europe, I had the conventional desire to make a lot of money, get rich, and enjoy the freedom that money brings. But all that changed. In Europe, I was frugal with everything, and the simplest discoveries blew my mind. I felt like I could be no richer. I pushed myself to have exceptional experiences that enriched me far more than I expected. I stayed in hostels for a few bucks a night and met other travelers in the same situation. I frequented grocery stores and bought lunch meat, bread, cheeses, and other functional items I needed to get through the day. Since I was traveling by myself, I could do what I wanted without worrying about anyone else. If I wanted to eat ham and cheese sandwiches on a park bench under the beautiful European sky, I could, and I often did just that for many of my meals.

My goal wasn't to spend as little as possible, but to get the most value out of what little money I had. As it turned out, the connections I made with new people provided the greatest value. During my first five days in Paris, I met a lot of tourists at the hostel where I stayed. Many of them were there for the short term while they looked for student apartments, and after those first five days, I didn't need the hostel anymore. A bunch of them found apartments and invited me to stay with them. This made me love traveling even more because I enjoyed rich experiences that didn't cost a lot of money, and it boosted my confidence that I could return home and live with this same outlook.

> My goal wasn't to spend as little as possible, but to get the most value out of what little money I had.

America provides tremendous opportunity, but for the first time I thought about the costs that are associated with wealth. Nice houses and cars require financing, debt, insurance, repair costs, and more. My entire European endeavor went against the grain of everything my parents wanted for my life and believed about theirs. And yet, so many wonderful things came out of it that changed our relationship forever. I realized that their strong opposition to my desires was rooted in fear about experiences they had not had and would, most likely, never have. As these incredible experiences poured into my life, my parents lost some authority to actively influence my life decisions.

We'd had our conflicts before, but it had never been so pronounced. I would always love Mom and Dad, but I was no longer afraid of disappointing them. I no longer felt pressured to live up to their standard.

In fact, I veered toward the opposite end of the spectrum. If something made my parents uncomfortable, that was my signal to pursue it.

I left everything. For months, I had planned, researched, networked, wrote, read, called, wondered, and dreamed. Finally, I got on the plane to Paris. I had never been out of the country by myself and had never started on a path that didn't have a certain outcome. I had always done what was expected, followed the rules, and received high marks. Now, I was doing what no one I knew had done, and what no one I knew expected me to do.

It was exhilarating!

On the plane, a woman who was a few years older sat next to me. We introduced ourselves and asked each other about our lives. I told her what I was doing, and when she asked me a few questions I detected a tone of disbelief, admiration—and maybe a little jealousy.

"I think you're gonna learn a lot about yourself," she said with a smile.

In my family, everyone had a purpose. If you were in school, you followed the rules, did your homework, listened to your teacher, and brought home good grades. The good report card was redeemed for free tokens at a Family Game Center, or a free personal pan pizza at Pizza Hut. If you played a sport, you practiced hard, listened to the coach, honed your skills, and cheered on your teammates. You did your best, and sometimes brought home a trophy.

If you did not study or play sports, you worked or looked for work. At your job, you adhered to the standards of the company, fulfilled the assignments, got to work on time, and did your best to earn your pay. Then you paid your share of tuition, gas, cars, etc. That was my life.

Now I was flying over the Atlantic Ocean, and on the way to ... what? There would be no school to attend, no sports to play, no job to do, and no teacher, coach, or boss to listen to. In my family's eyes, I was paying money to play. What was the purpose?

The truth was that I never knew the purpose. My purpose was to live without purpose and see what that felt like. Maybe I wasn't able to express it at the time, but perhaps the purpose was to answer the question *Who am I?*

If I had stayed at home, I would have latched on to whatever standard or purpose

> I had to get to a place where the environment and I did not know each other, so that we could explore and understand each other.

was put in front of me, or would have chosen one to pursue. I had to get to a place where the environment and I did not know each other, so that we could explore and understand each other. I was scared and nervous, but excited and eager to face the unknown.

Traveling alone empowered me because I had no one to answer to. For example, I wanted to visit the Grande Arc de la Defens, which sat several miles northwest of the center of Paris, so I took the subway to this famous structure that looks like a gigantic hollow cube. Paris is packed with structures and monuments like this one that demand that you find a seat and just observe, which I did.

"Look, it's Joe!" a female American voice said.

I turned around and saw a brown-haired girl and a taller guy, both with backpacks. I recognized their faces from the hostel, but couldn't remember their names.

"Hey there," I greeted them. "Isn't the Grand Arc incredible?"

"Totally," the guy said. "We're going downstairs to spend the day at the museum. Want to come with us?"

I scanned my mental checklist and assessed their invitation. Two people I didn't know asked me to go somewhere that I didn't want to see. My desire to please other people struggled against my resolve to make the best choices for myself.

"No thanks," I told them. "You two have fun, and I'll catch up with you at the hostel."

Maybe I expected them to make me feel bad about saying "no," but nothing happened.

"Cool," said the guy. "Have fun, man."

This wasn't the first time I said "no" to someone, but it was a memorable moment when I learned to be honest with myself and others, and to pay attention to what I wanted. I wanted to wander around by myself. With what I had gone through with the dorm fire and the counseling afterward, it took a lot for me to say "no" to them. Despite the inner angst I felt, they didn't seem to care a bit and wished me well. Their life went on. Without me. And my life would go on without them. Of all the places I visited and all the life-changing perspectives I gained, that brief moment meant so much.

Another such moment came in Madrid, Spain. I'd been traveling for a month and had always been lucky in terms of where I stayed, the sites I visited, and the trains I rode. That streak ended in Madrid.

I chose a low-end hostel because of the bargain rate and bought a three-day museum pass that gave me unlimited access to Madrid's biggest and most renowned museums. But my experience here was entirely different. At the hostel in Paris, there was a large common area where we socialized with other travelers, which made the value of the hostel greater than the cost. In Madrid, this bargain-basement hostel had dark, narrow hallways, dirty rooms, and no social area to generate connections. I was stuck by myself in a virtual dump with a grumpy owner to boot.

I visited the museums for a couple of days but didn't enjoy it. It was a big city, and I had no connections, no community, and little idea of where to go next. I had budgeted enough to stay there a full week, but I asked myself *What do I really want to do?*

I got out my map, and planned which direction I would head. My rail pass was for continental Europe only, and I still had plenty of time left to explore the mainland countries. I couldn't help but notice that Spain was near another country, but it wasn't in Europe. The only thing that separated me from exploring another continent was a train trip and ferry ride. I decided I would go to Africa the next day, and that decision was exhilarating. Not a soul in the world knew my exact location, and I felt alive and in control. I was far from home and completely out of my comfort zone, and I loved it.

While I traveled, I had plenty of time to think about what I wanted in life, and it changed my attitude about what I might do for work. I loved to travel, and I wanted whatever I did in the future to support that.

The lifestyles in Europe were so different from America, and I soaked it all up. In Spain, the stores both fascinated and frustrated foreigners because they closed their doors every afternoon for a siesta. A fellow backpacker told me that several European countries gave their employees two months of vacation. These two practices would be heresy in workaholic America. I knew on which side of the ocean I wanted to be.

I discovered that America was not the only reality, and it made me question the norms of our work environment and lifestyle. I knew I had to find a way to live in America with a European mindset toward the hours worked and time off. I had sampled unconventional employment in my sales role at Cutco, and I wanted to combine that type of success with an unconventional lifestyle. I could never be a cookie cutter, and when I came to that conclusion, the future seemed much more exciting. In fact, the fear of the unknown subsided, and the thrill of putting this puzzle together took over.

Chapter 8

From Kansas City to Kumamoto, Japan

When I got back to the US, I found I could not break all the bonds of my upbringing and pursue only the things I wanted. Before I went to Europe, I'd had my own sales office and sampled what life would be like in a management job. The job didn't set my heart aflutter, but because it resembled conventional employment and because I had not developed any kind of career plan whatsoever, I returned to that same position when I got home.

As my Europe adventure faded in the rear-view mirror, I fell back into sales mode. I was appalled by my unhappiness at work, and it seemed like a wish come true when I was offered a dream job. A friend of my sister's worked for a marketing company, and they specialized in cross-country tours where they promoted various products.

"I heard they have an opening," Lynn said.

"Do you know what the job is?" I asked. "I am up for learning something new, even if I can't do it yet."

"It's something about spring break and working on a beach in Florida."

"Working on a beach?" I said. "When can I talk to her?"

"I'll tell Andrea to call you."

Not long after, Andrea phoned me about the gig. "We're coordinating a spring break promotion with Dr Pepper," she said. "For four weeks, you'll be on Panama City Beach in Florida, running a beach cabana for Dr Pepper."

My head started to spin. "So what will I do?" I said.

"We'll have about two hundred beach chairs next to a bar that serves Dr Pepper. There will be games, contests, and giveaways every day. It's pretty cool."

"Sounds amazing. I have this other job right now, but let me check on things, and I'll call you soon."

"Make it quick. This is a last-minute position," she said.

Just like I had fallen back into my pre-Europe mindset about conventional employment, so had my dad. We sat out back in the same chairs where he had tried to talk me out of selling knives for Cutco and traveling to Europe. Now he wanted to talk me out of this unstable, temporary marketing opportunity.

"One month?" he said with exasperation. "What do you do after that?"

I stammered. "I-I don't really know yet. Maybe another marketing tour?"

"Do you know that for sure?"

"No, I just think this job would be fun."

"Fun? You've got to think of the long term, Joe. Seems like you've got a good structure in place here as a sales manager."

I hadn't listened to Dad before when he shot down my idea of backpacking through Europe, and that had worked out so well. But now he had legitimate concerns about something that, to me, sounded like an incredible opportunity. This time I gave him the benefit of the doubt.

"You're probably right," I said in surrender.

A few months later, I regretted that decision. Just a year after my incredible experience in Europe, I was living in Kansas City and slogging through a job as a sales manager. Life grew more miserable each week. I faced a mountain of business and personal debt, but worse than the money concerns, I had no direction and felt like I was out of options. I had dug a hole for myself that felt like a self-imposed prison. In one single year, I had gone from the mountaintop of freedom to the bottom of a dark canyon, barely surviving this daily grind. I felt trapped, lost, and rudderless.

Europe had set my heart on fire and taught me that I was responsible for my own happiness. I wanted that spark to get going again, and it came through my close friend Erica.

"You should teach English in Asia," she said, "My friend just got back from studying in Hong Kong, and she said that if you're a college graduate and speak English, you can make good money, travel, and have a good time over there."

That was all she knew about it, but it was enough to set my mind on fire like it had not been for a year. That same day, I started researching how I could teach English in Asia. I was ready to move mountains to get there.

Once I heard about Asia, any concerns I had about what my parents wanted were tossed out the window. Moving to Asia was like slaying the final villain in a video game. I don't mean that my parents were the bad guys, but through my past experiences, I realized that if I wanted to be happy, I had to focus on myself. To be happy, I had to stop making decisions according to what my parents wanted.

My idea of moving to Asia surprised them, not because I pursued it, but because this newest pursuit would be so grand. They asked me a few questions but never tried to talk me out of it. Or if they did, I don't remember it now.

Within a few weeks, I sent my application to the Japan Exchange and Teaching Program, or JET Program, so I could teach English in Japan. I told my bosses at Cutco that even though my next steps were not set in concrete, they should look for my replacement. With faith in the good things life would bring, I welcomed the next few months with open arms and asked life to provide an interesting path.

While all that was in motion, another opportunity cropped up. Andrea, my sister's friend from the marketing company, called again. They had an opening on one of their tours, and she offered me the job.

Within a week, I was in Tampa, Florida, promoting Campbell's Chunky Soup outside the Super Bowl. For two weeks, our group of twenty-somethings lived out of a hotel, traveled around the Tampa area in a bus that had once been used by the band 'NSync, handed out soup samples, ran games, and took the hectic job one day at a time. I had a microphone in my hands again, and I used it to get the crowd excited about a handful of free, cheap, sponge footballs. Super Bowl weekend slammed us with long hours that we spent on our feet. Waves of people arrived just to experience the atmosphere.

Ecstatic with our work, the company owners rewarded us with a party and told us that in a month, a new promotion in Panama City would begin. We would live on the beach for a month and entertain college kids on spring break. In between my old sales job and a total life change that would take place in Japan, this unconventional employment took me to unfamiliar and interesting environments.

The month in Panama City and all its shenanigans led to another gig: a two-month mobile tour of America. We followed a concert tour and promoted Spree Candy. We traveled about 20,000 miles in a vehicle that looked like nothing else on the road—a bright green SUV that served as a billboard for Spree Candy. These adventures brought me great happiness and, as great as they were, I knew I was on the brink of my next step—life in Asia.

After my application to JET was approved and I passed the interview process, I moved to Japan. I went to Kumamoto City on a one-year contract that was renewable for up to three years. I reveled in the fact that everything I had and did in my life was because of the decisions I'd made for myself. I didn't think I'd be in Japan forever, but I wanted to appreciate that time without worrying about what my next step would be. My parents were happy for my happiness, but sad about the distance between us.

When I love something, I want others to love it, too, so I talked to my brother, Mark, a few months after the school year started in Japan. "You graduate college next spring," I began. "I'm not going to say you're stupid if you don't join the JET Program," I said. "But please add it to your list of options."

"Okay," was all he said.

A few weeks later, when the application deadline was approaching, I hadn't heard back from Mark. I wished I had pushed him a little harder because it would have been great to experience Japan with my younger brother. Then he called.

"I got an interview with the JET Program," Mark said.

"I didn't even know you applied!" I said.

"After we talked, I filled out the application. We'll see what happens." My brother has always been a man of few words.

Not only was he accepted, but Mark's apartment was a fifteen minute bike ride from mine. We lived near each other in Kumamoto, Japan for two years and became closer than we had ever been. Everything we experienced was enhanced because we shared it as brothers.

Any foreigner who has spent time in Japan knows that it's customary for the Japanese to give compliments. To hear an insult or to be questioned about anything is rare, especially when a foreigner exhibits quirks.

A week before I went to Japan, a friend made a suggestion. "You should bleach your hair," he said.

"Why would I do that?" I asked.

"Because you're going to Japan. Why not?"

"Let's do it," I said.

For the first time ever, I allowed someone to change my entire hair color. I woke up the next morning with an obnoxious, platinum blonde head of hair. My future co-workers in Japan had only seen pictures of me, which featured my normal, natural brown hair. When we all met at the airport, they thought I was just another crazy American, so they shrugged it off. But a year and a half later, I had still not gotten a haircut, and I continued to bleach my hair every few months. My growing mane identified me to friends and students, who called me "Lion Sensei."

I knew my hair was an eyesore, but I wanted to push the envelope, as it were. I looked ridiculous. When my American friends back home saw photos of me, they mocked me and laughed at it. Mom sent three-word emails that said, "Cut. Your. Hair."

Mom sent three-word emails that said, "Cut. Your. Hair."

However, even at the peak of this chaos, the Japanese still complimented me. I had to find out just how ridiculous something had to become in order for them to come to their senses. What would prompt a Japanese person to say, "Why don't you cut that repugnant beehive off your head?"

Eighteen months into it, I was in New Zealand for Christmas vacation, where I went to a beachside hair salon. I went in with a blonde mess and came out with cornrows. A skilled artist, if you have enough hair, can braid it directly to the scalp in neat rows that look like orderly fields of corn. My hair was due for a bleaching, and the natural brown roots creeped toward the blonde ends, so my cornrows were brown at the scalp, but twisted and faded into yellow at the ends. It was quite a look.

The cornrows scored big with students and friends in Japan. Not only did a white guy with cornrows stick out, but a white guy with cornrows in Japan made heads turn. The cornrows stayed in for about a month, until they threatened to turn into dreadlocks. I was ready for it to unravel.

I decided to undo everything one night and assumed the process would take about fifteen minutes. Half an hour later, I was a tangled mess. I went out that night wearing a hat, resigned that I would have to shave my head the next day. But a tiny voice in my head assured me that something good would come of this. My good friend, Michiyo, a pretty Japanese girl with excellent English, had bleached my hair a few times before, and we ran into each other at a restaurant.

"Why are you wearing a hat?" she asked.

"I tried to take out my cornrows, but they got tangled," I told her. "I might have to shave my head."

"I could help you straighten it out."

"Really, you want to? Can you come over tomorrow and help me? We can either bleach everything again, or just shave it all off."

"Sure," she said. "See you then."

Michiyo arrived the next night and confirmed the chaos. "I can't help you," she said.

"I have an idea," I began. "Take these scissors and cut off the tangled parts. Leave everything else for now."

For about twenty minutes, she snipped away knots of tangled, half-done cornrows that were still braided to my scalp.

"I think that's everything," she concluded.

I turned to see my reflection in the glass cabinet in the kitchen, since the only mirror in the house was on the bathroom wall.

I had a mullet.

If you've never known the joy of mullets, a mullet is a haircut that appeared sometime in the late 1970s or '80s. First worn by soccer players in England, they spread across the world like a virus, looking like a dead animal. The hair is short on the top and the sides, with long hair that hangs down the back. Favored by such luminaries as American country music star Billy Ray Cyrus, English football emperor David Beckham, and various other celebrities over the years, they are now hopelessly out of style. Mullets have been called the Neck-warmer, the Missouri Compromise, the Business-Casual, the Texas Two-Step, and the Kentucky Waterfall.

What was now on my head was not your garden-variety mullet. All the bleached hair had been cut from the top and sides, but was prominent on the longer hair that fell down my back. I had a two-tone mullet.

From the front, my natural brown hair looked like a conventional haircut. From the side or back, you could see a shock of bleached hair that spilled down my back like a waterfall. In short, the business was brown, and the party was blonde!

This was going to be fun. My mullet would be the ultimate test in my social experiment. It was the definition of hideous. Would this prompt an insult in Japan?

I walked into school the next day and expected that people would laugh at my hair or ask me questions about it. The first person I saw was the assistant principal.

"Kakoii, Joe sensei! (Mr. Joe, you're so handsome!)" he said from across the teacher room.

Not only did his compliment stun me, it disappointed me! I couldn't look worse, but not one teacher or student said anything negative. Because it was different from the cornrows, they thought the change was cool!

Determined to get the most mileage out of the mullet, I went everywhere and begged to be mocked. I walked the Shimotori and Kamitori, which were covered mall-like walkways downtown. I worked the door at Sharp's, the well-known gathering spot for foreigners in Kumamoto. I introduced myself to an elementary class and even took the time to teach them the concept of a mullet.

"Short-long," I said to thirty second graders. "Please repeat."

"Short. Long," they replied in unison.

"Now say, 'Joe's hair is mullet.'" It came out "Ma-retto," and I giggled for the entire class period.

That mullet lived and breathed for nine glorious days and was documented on video, film, and in print. On the ninth day, one of the junior high students approached me. Miwa greeted me every day with her sweet smile and simple English. I assumed she drew the short straw for who should tell the American teacher that his hair should be set out with the other bags of trash. Miwa's words were measured, intentional, and unmistakable.

"Joe-sensei," Miwa began, and waved to me from the entrance of the teacher's room.

"Good morning, Miwa," I said, and motioned her to come to my desk.

She spoke a full sentence, but each word came out as a question.

"Now? You are? Nice guy?" she said with a smile and an energetic thumb up. She continued.

"But? If? You?" Miwa put her hands behind her head and made a caressing motion. "Cut?" She paused, then ended with an even bigger smile and two emphatic thumbs up. "VERY NICE GUY."

That was it. The mullet had run its course. A fifteen-year-old Japanese girl didn't quite say that my hair was painful to look at, but she made her point. I had pushed the envelope to see how long it would take to burst. The answer was nine days. That very night, Michiyo and I shaved my head.

The mullet experience not only became a favorite story to tell for the rest of my life, it also led to a relationship that would last. Michiyo and I started dating the day she fashioned my mullet. I figured that if this woman could appreciate me at my most unattractive time, we had a bright future together. I was right, and about a year later, we were engaged.

After Mark moved to Japan, it was pretty hard for my parents to have two sons so far away, and Mom sent me an email about how Dad felt.

"Your father was hoping to have a bigger part in your lives at this point," she wrote.

I wanted Mom and Dad to be happy but learned that they could not dictate my life's happiness. It took a while, but I would eventually arrive at the place Dad wanted me to be. Thankfully, it was on my terms.

In the summer between my second and third year in Japan, I decided to skip a trip home to America because I could save some money and maximize further travel in Asia. Oddly enough, my focus on international travel brought me around to a greater appreciation for home.

> Oddly enough, my focus on international travel brought me around to a greater appreciation for home.

Before the school term started, a friend and I planned to take the short flight from Japan to Seoul, Korea. We had both been there before and wanted to get out of Japan without going too far away. Korea was perfect for that, and we had a good time together until my friend had to leave a few days earlier than me. I decided to do some exploring on my own.

I picked up a guidebook, and a picture of white-water rafting caught my eye. I decided to check it out and boarded a train. A few hours outside the safe confines of Seoul, Korea's largest city, I boarded a bus and entered a town in the mountains as described in the guidebook.

This town was in the middle of the countryside, and the people seemed really unhelpful. There were no foreigners or English speakers, and I concluded that this was not a tourist hotbed. Someone in a hotel finally directed me to a bus that would take me to another town that might offer some tourist activities.

I was struck by a moment of clarity. I had no real place to go or person with whom to connect, and I missed home. I was homesick. I'd had that feeling plenty of times before, but this time the feeling was overwhelming. My heart was telling me that I needed to go home for a taste of time with my family.

I hadn't been back to St. Louis in an entire year and wouldn't get a chance to go home for at least six more months. I thought about how some people go to prison for a shorter time than that. All I could think about was my parents and my family. I knew I had to get home for Christmas, but I also began to think about my life after Japan. I still wanted to see the world, but my family was the most important thing to me. On that bus in the Korean mountains, I decided that I wanted to live near the people I loved, in the place where I was raised.

I got off at the next stop, returned to the main town, and caught a train back to Seoul. The next day I flew back to Japan and started planning my trip home for Christmas. I only had one more year to teach. I had no idea what would come after that, but now I knew where I wanted to live.

Chapter 9

You do What?
You PLAY For a Living?

My time in Japan had ended, and Michiyo and I had finalized our union at the courthouse. We signed the papers and sealed the deal, but we had to start the process of getting Michiyo a visa/green card. We planned to have wedding day celebrations in both Japan and America, and each of us would handle the details in our own country.

Michiyo did her part, and the wedding day in Japan was smooth and perfect. Now I had to step up and deliver for our American celebration. I called a DJ company to book the entertainment for our reception and asked about details. The woman on the phone described what they did.

"It sounds like DJs have a pretty fun job," I said.

"You sound like you have the personality for it," she said. "Why don't you come on board with us?"

I was taken aback, but encouraged. "Let's see how your DJ does at our reception first," I said. A seed had been planted.

I could not have been more impressed with our DJ and his job. Keith Robinson amazed everyone from start to finish. The night began with a high-spirited introduction of the wedding party in the style of the classic Chicago Bulls' introductions from the 1990s.

"And now, the starting lineup for your wedding party!" Keith began. He ran through personal introductions for each bridesmaid and groomsman.

He kept everything flowing, from the toasts and dinner to cake cutting and spotlight dances. Once the dancing started, he kept the dance floor packed, and his mix of music, based on our preferences and requests, kept the guests jumping and dancing all night. The apex of the party came toward the end, when Michiyo's parents were coaxed to the dance floor for "Pour Some Sugar on Me." Keith handed out some inflatable guitars, and Michiyo's dad, a tiny, straight-faced Japanese businessman, grabbed that guitar and absolutely rocked it out. For the grand finale, Keith got everyone in a circle around Michiyo and me to send us off.

"Repeat after me," he said, which the crowd did. "Thank you. For letting us. Be a part of your big day. No matter where you go. No matter what you do. You will always. Have family and friends who love you. Oh and by the way. Next year for Thanksgiving. We're coming to your place."

Everyone cheered, and Keith ended with, "Group hug everybody!!!"

The entire group collapsed in on us as Keith blasted the final song. A ball of energy exploded on the dance floor, and the party ended in triumph.

A job as a DJ fit every requirement in which I envisioned myself. Because I lived for joyous gatherings of happy people, I couldn't imagine anything better than serving a prominent role in one of the most important days in a family's life. As a wedding DJ, I could be myself and speak to the crowd, participate in a fun party, plus get a paycheck! After the music ended and the lights came on, I approached Keith.

"Great job Keith, thank you so much! How can I do this?" I asked.

"Let me pack up my stuff here," he said. "And let's talk soon."

A month later, Keith was training me.

When I began to let happiness and passion dictate my decisions, I felt at peace with myself and my life. It's not easy to forge unexplored paths, but every experience built my confidence that things would work out well. I knew I would learn valuable lessons either way.

I learned that the more I say "yes" to things that don't matter, the more I will continue to do things that don't matter. When I learned to say "yes" to the right things instead of doing things that weren't aligned with my heart's desires, my happiness increased.

When Michiyo and I moved back to America, we lived with my parents for a time. I was working as a DJ but had not found or even looked for steady work. Our neighbor

I learned that the more I say "yes" to things that don't matter, the more I will continue to do things that don't matter.

ran a car repair shop, and one day he saw me in the front yard and called me over.

"If you need work, I can offer you a position in the office," he said.

"Thanks," I said. "I think I'll pass right now, but I'll keep it in mind."

Even though we had little income, I resolved that whatever I did, it would either be very enjoyable, feature high pay, involve people, or all of the above.

For the first time, I got paid to be on the microphone and entertain large groups of people as a DJ. The money was not great, but Saturday nights were so much fun. One day the boss called me in for a conversation.

"Joe, you haven't been doing this long," he began, "but you're doing a great job with us."

"Thank you," I told him. "I'm having a blast."

"Have you considered a career with our company?"

I was silent for a few moments. Besides my fellow DJs, I didn't know anything about what went on in the office and had no desire to learn. To humor him, I played along.

"Tell me what you mean," I said.

"You'd be around the office more and get more involved with sales," he explained. "On Saturday nights, you could go to two or three parties to evaluate and work with the other DJs."

"So let me get this straight," I said as I stifled a chuckle. "You're asking to take the mic out of my hand?"

"Well, if you look at it that way."

"That's why I wanted to DJ in the first place. And it's why I like this so much. I am flattered at your offer, but I'll pass for now."

Over time, I got better at saying "yes" to opportunities that fit my criteria for happiness. I always had a positive outlook, and also enjoyed the peace that came from how I spent my time and how I made a living. That's made me feel that much better about everything.

I love to help other people pursue the things that make them happy. That feeling, for me, is similar to being on stage. I want to

> That's what I do: I challenge myself and challenge others to challenge themselves.

do all I can to help other people to have a fun and fulfilling life, one that may be a bit unconventional but tailor-made for what they love. That's what I do: I challenge myself and challenge others to challenge themselves. That's a lot of challenging.

Michiyo and I settled into a humble apartment outside of downtown St. Louis. We filled in the blanks of married life as best we could. She took a job as a preschool teacher, and I worked on Friday and Saturday nights as a DJ. The perfect union of our job requirements and our personal talents led to early success but did not provide the paychecks to match. I now had a family to support, even if that family consisted of only two people.

I was proud that I hadn't settled for a cubicle and a paycheck, but I soon found out that people cannot dine on happiness alone. And since most people don't get married on weekdays, I searched for another job to supplement being a DJ.

An ad in the paper led me to another unconventional position: a magician. As a kid, I had read about magic tricks in library books, but I never got around to doing anything with them. Now that interest resurfaced.

A small company called Abra-Kid-Abra put on after-school classes and summer camps, and we taught elementary students skills in magic and circus. I took to the job right away and became a performer and salesperson for our programs.

During the week, I learned, taught, and performed magic and circus skills, and on weekend nights, I was a DJ and entertained celebratory crowds of several hundred people. No one had ever suggested I become a DJ who juggled and did magic, but within a few months of moving home, I was getting paid to do the things that really made me happy.

It was fulfilling, and as for freedom, Michiyo and I managed to travel quite a bit. We ignored the normal custom of spending one or two weeks at an expensive, island resort for our honeymoon and made our way across a new continent instead. We planned a two-month jaunt across South America—from Rio de Janeiro, Brazil, to Lima, Peru, and in between—and we went to Uruguay, Argentina, and Bolivia. A year after that, we spent two months on an around-the-world trip. That dream trip included several weeks in Turkey, Egypt, India, Korea, and an entire month in Japan.

When I started my career as an entertainer, the goal was to continue until I couldn't pay the bills anymore. Michiyo went along with the plan, and we both expected it would last two or three years. When my work hours became weekend nights, our quality time together decreased, but we knew it was only for two or three years and were willing to make that sacrifice. The more often I got on stage, behind a mic, or in front of a crowd, the better I became. I had found my passion, and didn't want to do anything else.

Next step: baby. We were blessed with a healthy, hilarious son we named Hiroki. When he turned three, we learned that Michiyo was pregnant with our second child. The news was exciting, but the pregnancy was not.

Her first trimester was pure torture. Morning sickness would have been welcome, but Michiyo was nauseous for entire days at a time. She had to sleep and relax a lot because too much physical activity made her throw up. Worse than that, her nausea was triggered by the smell of any food.

As she suffered through these physical ailments, my stress and frustration increased. Besides taking care of our son, I had to handle all the details of our life such as paying bills, shopping, and preparing meals. Plus I had to work. My frustration was that I was helpless to relieve my wife's discomfort.

The only thing that could cure her was time, which seemed to crawl slower than a turtle. The stress was extreme and inescapable. I felt like a man snowed in for the entire winter, and I needed a sliver of hope or inspiration to keep me sane. My sister, Katie, helped straighten some things out.

"Beside the stress at home, what's driving you right now?" she asked.

"Every single day is so rough," I said. "I need something to shoot for that will pull me through this."

"You're doing a lot of cool things. Can't one of them be the thing you're looking for?"

"I love being a DJ, magician, and juggler. I never imagined I could do this stuff for my job. I just feel like there's something else I am ignoring."

Katie asked a key question. "What is the one thing you would do if you knew you couldn't fail?"

I hesitated to share my answer with her, so I started with a story. "One of my idols is this guy, Patrick Combs. He's a motivational speaker, and he came to my college once. He wrote a book, and I read it. He's done some cool things. I have always wanted to be that."

"A motivational speaker?"

"Yes. I want to be a motivational speaker."

She thought about that for a few minutes. I loved talking to my sister because we could share anything with comfort and without judgment.

"Then you have to do it," she said with finality.

"What do you mean?" I said.

"If that's the thing, then you have to go for it."

"Yeah, but I don't really know what to do."

"Do something. Take some small action toward that. Use that as the light at the end of this tunnel. If you can do it now when things are most difficult, think of what you can do when everything gets better."

Katie was spot on. I had to take action in the direction I wanted to go.

"You're right, Sis. Thank you so much. I'm going be a speaker," I told her.

I gathered a few photos and video clips of my travels and other visual treasures, and I made a modest, two-minute video about What Joe Fingerhut Does. I explained what I could do for audiences, and the video ended with " Visit www.joefingerhut.com." I didn't even own that domain name yet. I watched that video every night for two months, and every day I researched other speakers' web sites and videos to get more ideas.

I knew I needed a jump-start. For several years, I had gotten emails about a conference in California that was about the business of speaking. It would not be cheap, and I talked to Michiyo about it. She sat at the kitchen table, one hand on her stomach, one hand on her forehead.

"This won't be easy, but if I don't do this now, I may never do it," I said.

"Then go to California," she said. And then she went back to bed.

The conference opened my eyes, and what I learned and the people I met gave me the confidence I needed to pursue professional speaking. Two weeks later, I did a magic show for a group of adults. At the end, two women told me about their youth conference and asked if I entertained for that kind of thing. A few days later, they hired me. Then my cousin who taught seventh grade invited me to his middle school, where I spoke to the outgoing eighth grade class.

I still did magic shows and DJ gigs to pay the bills. Michiyo improved, and we soon had a healthy baby girl. Over the course of just a few months, I had turned my dream of being a motivational speaking into a reality.

The life I had only thought possible was coming to fruition. The funny thing is that the longer I kept myself in a position to do unconventional things, the more often unconventional opportunities found me.

> The funny thing is that the longer I kept myself in a position to do unconventional things, the more often unconventional opportunities found me.

Occasionally, I fell into the trap of comparing myself to others. I looked at my friends' jobs and salaries, and an occasional small whisper of regret crept in. That voice told me that I should have settled for more conventional employment with tangible, conventional benefits. Those feelings usually didn't last long because I learned to turn them around with a phone call to a prospective client who just might hire me as a speaker. Then I'd snap back to my immense gratitude that my bills were paid, and I'd have a renewed appreciation for the variety in my work.

My move to Asia set me on the path to make decisions that satisfied my own needs, rather than those of my parents, and they accepted my decisions. When I moved back, my generally conservative parents thought my path was interesting at best, insane at worst. They never thought that their oldest son would support himself and his new wife as a part-time DJ who taught magic on the side and traveled a few weeks out of the year. That son, however, became his own man, made his own right decisions, and was more than capable of handling whatever consequences arose. And now my parents are strong supporters of everything I pursue.

My parents and I have a deep appreciation for our past because we've traveled a long, windy road together. Some of our best moments are when we sit around and tell stories from "the good old days" when Mom and Dad couldn't wrap their head around what I was thinking, and vice versa. One of my favorite quotes is from Mark Twain that seems to sum it up:

> When I was fourteen, I thought my Dad knew nothing. By the time I turned twenty-one, he had learned quite a bit.

Part II

NO MORE EXCUSES:

How To Slay The "I Can't" Dragon, So You Can Get What You Want

Excuse 1

I Don't Know What I Want To Do With My Life

In high school, I worried about a lot of things, but I agonized about what I would pick for my college major. Those worries vanished after a brief conversation with my second grade gym teacher. Miss Shannon had been one of my favorite teachers, and my mom and I ran into her at a school event.

"Tell me what to study in college," I said to Miss Shannon.

"What do you want to do?" she asked.

"That's the problem. I don't know yet, and I'm worried about picking the wrong thing."

"Don't worry about it, Joe," she said. "Remember two things: (1.) Seventy to eighty percent of college graduates don't work in their field of study, and (2.) The average person changes careers six to seven times."

What? That was news to me. Neither my parents, my guidance counselors, nor my teachers had ever told me this, and I thought about those two statistics a lot.

If most people don't get a job that matches their degree, what was so important about picking a major? I knew I liked several subjects, including math, English, gym, and lunch, but others, like biology, chemistry, physics, and pretty much anything in science, didn't interest me.

And why did people change careers so often? Both my parents started out as teachers, and then Dad went into computer programming and stuck with it for thirty years. That was my template. But if what Miss Shannon told me was true, that meant Mom and Dad were not normal (which wouldn't be the last time that thought struck me). I reasoned that people switched careers because they weren't happy and wanted to find something better.

I decided not to stress too much about my major, since the odds of not working in that field were excellent. Later on, I was never afraid to try a new job or career because I knew it didn't have to be permanent. Miss Shannon planted a seed that night. My own happiness could be my guide for making career and life decisions. If change was inevitable, I wanted to be as happy as possible in any given situation.

Here's the reality: The vast majority of people are just like I was. They don't know what they want to do when they grow up. They might think they have to do the kind of work their parents did, which probably means working at a conventional job that has conventional hours—with only a little happiness. People seem to gravitate toward what they know, and some kids may look at their parents' work and think they have to do the same thing, even if they don't like it.

It's a twofold problem. We sell ourselves short when we don't put in the work to explore all of our options, and when we find something we like, we don't take action and pursue it. Too many people think it's beyond their reach to go after the kind of work that would make their heart sing. Even worse, they may think they don't deserve it.

Remember that nothing is permanent. Want to be a professional athlete? Eventually, you'll get old and won't perform like you used to. Want to be a movie star? Your body, voice, and appearance will change, as will your popularity. Heck, the President of the United States only has the job for four years, eight if things go well. Want to be a parent? One day you'll be chasing the kids around, and a decade later you'll come home to an empty house. Life, people, and careers are in a constant state of change.

Even people who seem to have it all together can have their doubts. A college friend, Eric, was one of those people. He was smart, good looking, ran cross-country, and had a great personality—and he was headed to med school. During our final semester, we caught up with each other.

"Are you excited about med school?" I asked.

"Oh, didn't you hear?" he said. "I'm not going."

"What! You made it this far, dude! You survived the 'weed-out' courses. I heard you actually liked Organic Chemistry. Nobody likes Organic Chemistry!"

"Med school . . . it just isn't for me. I don't know what I'm going to do now."

Eric now lives on a self-sustaining farm in Virginia. He had it all together, he really did, and then he changed his path so he could follow his heart.

If you think of life as an exploration, it becomes so much more interesting! If you think of yourself as a detective, the feelings of dread and confusion about your future will be minimized, and you can open yourself up to the adrenaline and endorphin rush of discovering new possibilities.

If you think of life as an exploration, it becomes so much more interesting!

The detective approach

The easiest way to learn about different options, and quite frankly, the cheapest, is to talk to other people. The more people you engage, the more information you receive, and the more possibilities you'll discover. The great thing about people is that they all have different ideas, and they all like to talk about themselves.

To open up the conversation, start with this question: *Could you share your experiences with me?* You may have to sit through some unnecessary babble, but be patient. Everyone has had a unique life, and something they share could be of tremendous value to you.

I love to learn about what other people have done, who they've met, and what they've learned. Learning about other people is fun. I've always had the gift of gab, but what that actually means is that I listen. People don't want to hear about you, they want to tell you what they know. And if you let them do most of the talking, they'll often tell you how much they enjoyed the conversation. To learn a lot, become a good listener.

You already know that I like to save my money, which is another reason why I LOVE talking to people. It doesn't cost a thing! New ideas and new energy flows when we make new connections. At the store, in a waiting room, even with a customer service rep on the other end of the phone, there are golden nuggets just waiting to be discovered. It's your job to find these nuggets. So ask questions.

If you keep your dreams locked in your heart, that's where they will die. Dreams are like babies. They can't stay inside you forever. Your dreams need oxygen to live and space to grow. No one can read your mind, and they cannot see inside your heart. You have to let them out. Tell other people about your dreams and desires, and describe them in detail. Just like it takes a village to raise a child, you cannot nurture your dreams by yourself. You need other people behind you.

> Dreams are like babies. They can't stay inside you forever. Your dreams need oxygen to live and space to grow.

Loyola University had a campus in Rome, and every single friend of mine went to study there during the second semester of our sophomore year—except me. As the clock ticked toward graduation, I realized that I had never been out of the country and might miss my only chance. The only solution was to study in Rome, but in order to do so, I'd have to extend my college career by at least one semester. I came up with a plan where I would complete the classes I needed to fulfill my major during my senior year, then take an extra semester in Rome.

Dad was not on board with this plan. Big surprise. Dad said that an extra semester would cost a lot of money. Why should I pay full tuition if I'd already completed my degree?

My goal was to get out of the country, and I had to find a way to do it without the expense of school. Was it even possible? Who could I talk to?

I told my friend, Matt, that I wanted to go to Europe after graduation. "My uncle did that," he said in a dry tone.

I latched onto that comment. "What do you mean?" I asked.

"After college, he went to Europe."

I shot questions at him faster than he could answer and begged to know more. "Was he rich?"

"No."

"Was he in school?"

"No."

"Did he have a job?"

"No."

"Did he know somebody?"

"No."

"WHAT DID HE DO?!" I demanded.

"I don't know," he said. "He just went."

Another seed was planted. If Matt's uncle could do it, so could I. I didn't know how, but now I had proof that it could be done.

I started talking to everyone about my trip. Most people didn't have any helpful information about how to go to Europe without being in a study program, but I still played the odds and told everyone about my goal. The problem was that my community consisted of young people who had little experience and none outside the study abroad program. That didn't fit my needs, but I kept talking.

My friend, Katie, was a happy Green Bay Packers fan from Wisconsin. We had met a few years earlier, and she became that one friend who greeted every story with a smile, every joke with a laugh, and every dream with a pat on the back.

"Katie, I'm going to Europe," I told her.

"Really? What do you mean?" she asked.

"After graduation, I am going to find a way to go to Europe. It's my dream. I just don't know how to do it," I said.

"My cousin just gave me a book about that."

"About Europe?" I asked.

"Yeah, it's about how to backpack and do things really cheap," she said.

My heart raced. "Do you have it? Can I see it?"

She reached to her bookshelf and pulled out a thin paperback with a white cover and bold, black letters on the front. *Europe On 84 Cents A Day* by Gil White. The title sounded too good to be true! I opened it up and skimmed through the table of contents.

Chapter 1: How to get around affordably in Europe

Chapter 2: How to stay affordably in Europe

Chapter 3: How to eat affordably in Europe

The list went on and on and seemed to address almost every concern I had.

"Katie, this is a miracle!" I yelled.

"Whatever. It's just a book, Joe," she said.

"This is the answer! This is what I have been looking for!"

"Great. It's yours," she said, happy she could provide something useful.

I studied that book, read it cover to cover, and referenced the content often over the next few months. That book ended up being my guide throughout my European experience.

If I had kept my dream to myself, I would never have left the country. Instead, I talked to as many people as possible about my vision and asked them what and who they knew. I made my dream happen because I connected with other people, and it changed my life. I had learned the first step of turning a goal into a reality. If I wanted answers, I had to scatter my intentions out to the world, so the answers could find me.

"You should teach English in Asia."

The moment my friend, Erica, said those words, my whole mindset changed. At the time, I lived in an apartment in Kansas City and had attempted to start a business, with a major emphasis on the word *attempt*. Just one year earlier, I had been deep in bliss in the middle of Europe with my backpack. Now, I was back home slogging along in a job I hardly cared about, and I worked without any goal other than to make some money. My life had turned into everything I'd wanted to avoid: job, bills, BORING! My heart was far away in a backpack in Europe, and I knew something major had to change to pull me out of that rut.

Erica and I had grown close over the last few years. We'd shared each other's ups and downs, and she had been supportive of my trip to Europe. She could see that I was not only open to, but desperate for, a way out.

"You should teach English in Asia," she said in a casual tone.

"What?" I asked. "You're not serious."

"My friend, Jen, just got back from studying in Hong Kong, and she said there's lots of foreigners that have finished school and are teaching

English there," she told me. "They make good money, get to travel around, and have lots of fun."

I was in. Now I had to figure out how to do it.

My roommate saw how enthusiastic I was and wanted to help me. "What exactly do you want from an experience in Asia?" he asked.

"It's not a long list," I said. "My goal is to live and teach English in an Asian country."

"Okay, so what are your requirements?"

"I don't want to volunteer or work for low pay," I said. "Nothing against volunteering, I just don't want to do that right now."

"Good start," he said. "So money is important?"

"Yes," I answered. "I'm almost out of debt, and I really want to start saving. If I don't make much, I can't save much."

"Makes sense. Is money the main thing?" he asked.

"No, the main thing is to explore and experience other cultures. I want to love life while I am there, to find a way to travel around and see even more places."

"And make some money while you're doing it?"

"Exactly," I said.

"Better get on the internet and make some connections," he suggested.

I soon found a site called Dave's ESL Cafe. ESL means English as a Second Language. ESLcafe.com has now become one of the most reliable, in-depth resources for those who want to teach English in various parts of the world, but at that time, it was still pretty basic.

I started reading the forums because I wanted to hear from people who were already working in other countries, and these people were located in every corner of the earth. They made it clear that if I could speak English, I could teach English in practically any country in the world.

And they were so open and accessible. Many of them listed their email addresses in their posts, and they offered their input and expertise. I introduced myself to several of them and asked for their advice about building a life and career in Asia. Most of them encouraged me to go for it and even suggested other web sites and resources to consider. Through these interactions, I expanded my perspective and learned how to gather more information, so I could make the right decisions.

My initial contract with JET would be for one year, but it could be renewed for up to three years. That was exactly what I wanted. Japan was a whole different world to soak in, explore, and embrace. After two months, I knew I would stay the full three years.

At the time, my brother was a senior in college, and I suggested he look into JET himself. He applied, interviewed, and accepted their offer. After he graduated, he moved to an apartment ten minutes from mine, and we spent two years traveling to Vietnam, New Zealand, Hong Kong, and all over Japan together.

My experience in Japan confirmed that when my mind was open to new possibilities, and I took action to pursue those opportunities, anything was possible. I didn't know what life would be like on the other side of the world, nor did I know how to make that happen. But when I took action to research and pursue this possibility, extraordinary things happened that still affect almost every part of my perspective and outlook.

Now if an opportunity or experience intrigues me, I do a little research to find out more about it. I ask, *How can I make this happen? How do people make this work in their lives? Is it a good fit for my life?* The information is available, and all you have to do is reach out, find it, and if it matches up with your dreams, act on it.

The magic of a list

According to The National Science Foundation, the average person has about 50,000 thoughts in a typical the day. Is it any wonder that we find it difficult to focus on one particular goal, let alone several? Sometimes we see the trees, but not the forest. At other times we see the forest but forget about the trees. And then there are times when our focus jumps back and forth from the trees to the forest like a ping-pong ball.

In order to build and keep your focus, the first step to is to make a list of your ideas and the associated tasks. A pen and paper are powerful tools to help sort out the spaghetti mess of thoughts in your head. When you write things down, it establishes a starting point for the numerous tasks that build upon each other and are crucial to get you to the next step. You can only hold one thought at a time, therefore, if you don't write things down, you spend a lot of energy trying to remember them. A written list frees your mind to analyze and evaluate important things—like what to do with your life.

Your list becomes your guide for actionable steps. For example, if you need to get your oil changed, several steps are involved:

- travel time to an oil change place
- wait time for the service
- conversation with the mechanic or clerk that could involve additional repairs
- payment for the services

That's a pretty simple list, but if your dream is something big, like teaching in Asia, where on earth would you start? A list will help you focus on the next best action, whether that is conducting research online or at a library or seeking advice from other people. And don't be surprised if one item morphs into a separate list of its own. When you take consistent action toward your tasks, you will gather additional information about important things to consider and precautions to take.

A list is also rewarding! Every time you cross something off, you'll have tangible proof that you are moving toward your goal. Not only will you feel a sense of satisfaction and closure as you check off the items, but you prioritize the most important ideas and tasks.

After Erica planted the seed that I could teach English in Asia, I had to decide where to go. Asia has a ton of countries and stretches across two hemispheres. I wanted to be in the Eastern part, but I didn't know much about that area. In fact, if I had been given a blank map, I would have known only a handful of countries.

I narrowed it down to four countries. I had studied Mandarin Chinese in high school, so China made the cut, as well as Taiwan, where Mandarin is spoken. Ever since I saw the movie "Karate Kid II," Japan had intrigued me. Plus Nintendo and plenty of other electronic stuff came from there. Finally, Thailand made my list and had been locked in my brain since a girl in Amsterdam described it to me as a vacation paradise.

I sought input from people at ESL Café to make the best possible decision, and I put all my effort toward that. Here are some samples of their helpful forum posts.

Taiwan and Japan seemed like they would be the best first-world alternatives.

Bingo! This was exactly what I wanted to know.

A few weeks later, my roommate asked, "Did you decide where you're going to go?"

"I'm going to apply for the JET Programme in Japan," I said. "If Japan doesn't work out, I'll head to Taiwan and see what I can generate there."

I applied and was accepted with JET and learned that my new home would be in Kumamoto, Japan. Just like it had been with Europe, my dream of living in a new place came true, and I moved to a country where I knew not one single person, nor the language.

I still use this same decision-making process to guide me in making other important decisions. Whenever I'm faced with a new possibility or a new idea, making a list helps me evaluate each opportunity. Whether it is a job I thought was impossible or a trip to a place I've never known, writing down my thoughts leads to making lists, which produces facts and informed decisions. It also keeps me accountable to my progress and is a source of ideas to reconsider.

EXCUSE BUSTER:

Embrace the dream you hold in your heart and create an initial plan to pursue it!

Ask:

1. Write down several skills or jobs you'd like to explore. You aren't committed to DO them or master them at this point. The goal is to learn more about them.
2. Who can you talk to about this to learn more?
3. How can other people help you discover what your dream job might be?
4. Name something you want to do that is so important to you that you could ditch the fear of being ridiculed or being scolded and tell someone. Who will you tell?
5. Picture your dream life. What kind of work would it include? What kind of activities or tasks would be involved? Write them down.
6. Now write down the kind of activities or tasks you do NOT want in your life.
7. How can you incorporate the things you love into your work, while avoiding the things you don't like?
8. How have other people done this? Who inspires you?

Act:

1. Make a list of steps you can take that will put you on the path to a job that will be support your dream life.
2. Pick one and DO IT!

Excuse 2

My Parents Want Me To Do Something Different

Matt Damon, the famous actor, once gave an interview about being a parent. I usually shrug off celebrity opinions because their expertise is in the entertainment field, rather than parenting, politics, or other issues. However, Matt Damon's response struck a chord, and it reminded me of the deep love a parent feels toward their children. Here's my paraphrased version: "I never fathomed that there would be a human in my life for whom I would give my own life," he said. "But that feeling has been with me since the moment my daughter was born."

I am not an action movie star or an Oscar-winning actor with vast riches. Most people do not fit that category and can't relate to it. But I can relate to being a parent.

Parents have the best interests of their kids at heart. With all the love and material things our parents provide us for the first few decades of our lives, it is understandable that we want to make them proud. We want them to know that their direction and care has shaped us.

It gets complicated when it comes time to make our own decisions. On one hand, we want to please our parents, who have invested so much in us for so long. We can never repay them for that, nor would they want us to. On the other hand, we must please the person in the mirror.

In my opinion, most parents hope their children will have a safe, dependable, full-time job. They'd prefer that their child sit in a cozy and snug office, earning benefits and vacation, living somewhere near their original family. The problem is that, for a young person who needs to get to know themselves, that's about as interesting as waiting for water to boil.

Embrace the difference!

When your parents aren't on board with what you want to do, the best strategy—which will pay immediate dividends—is to embrace their perspective. Conversation etiquette dictates that, in polite society, you don't talk about politics or religion because it's likely to end up in conflict. It's practically impossible to change someone else's opinion, particularly when they're invested in it.

Kids face a similar situation with their parents. At some point, your desires will conflict your parents' point of view. Both you and your parents may think, "If they could just see it my way, there wouldn't be a problem." But if both sides will let go of that hope and not only accept, but embrace the difference in perspectives, you'll have a better chance of reaching a solution.

Understand the parental point of view (it's not impossible!)

Your parents' perspective must be understood in context, which means that you need to understand their background, their experiences, and their values. When your difference in age is twenty or thirty years, that gap represents a world of change. Parents can be set in their ways and accustomed to following the principles of how they were raised, and they adapt their own conclusions and opinions based on that. Teenagers, on the other hand, do not have nearly the same life experience. They are still forming their life views, testing their limits, and learning to understand their place in the world.

When you understand what's behind your parents' perspectives, you can often find common ground. The direct approach is probably the best way to find out about their past. Ask them about it! Ask them about what life was like when they were your age, and get them to tell you about their experiences at various ages that helped shape their opinions.

When you open up to honestly communicate with your parents, the barrier between you can start breaking down, or can at least be minimized to a workable scenario. It can lead to a partnership together, where both your opinions look to better the other. This dual-focus prevents a wedge from forming, which benefits everyone in the long run.

Dad was not down with Europe

From the moment I told Dad about my plan to study in Europe without the studying, he was one hundred percent against it. He peppered me with questions and did not mince words.

"It's a pipe dream, and it's not gonna happen," he said.

He broke my dream apart and had me in tears, but I never gave up on it. I realized that I needed to talk about going to Europe *on Dad's terms.* I would find a way to get to Europe, but I also valued my relationship with my parents. They didn't have to support me, but I didn't want to jeopardize our long-term relationship by going against their wishes.

Dad shot down my first idea about traveling and studying abroad. When I discovered the backpacker approach, I picked up the conversation again.

"Dad, I found a way to go to Europe," I told him one day.

"I thought we already talked about this," he said.

"We talked about studying abroad. I found a way to go that doesn't involve school."

He sighed. "Fine. What are you thinking now?"

"I think I'll backpack around Europe. I read a book about how to travel without spending much money. Cheap hotels, travel by train, stuff like that."

"What about all the things we talked about? Those concerns haven't changed."

I remembered. He was talking about my safety, my lack of language skills, and his fear that when I got back all the good jobs would be taken.

"I'll figure it out," I said.

"You're going to have to show me you're ready."

"Fine. What do you want me to do?"

We had a reasonable conversation, and it helped us both in a big way. I had to accept the fact that Dad—who has a Masters degree in

Math—is a logical thinker. He focuses on details, safety mechanisms, and backup plans. But I'm more of a dreamer, eager to seize an idea and take action, and I just expect that all the pieces will fall into place. I embraced these differences.

His first main concern was the budget.

"You need to make sure you have enough money before, during, and after the trip," he said.

"That's a good point," I said, actually surprised at how much sense that made.

"Of course it's a good point! You have to save enough before you leave, so you can go over there with some money, and you have to make sure that you have enough while you are there, especially if something happens."

"What could possibly happen?"

Dad gave a patient, frustrated smile, and shook his head. "Joe, anything could happen. And we won't be able to fly over to come get you."

"That hadn't even occurred to me," I said. And it hadn't. I never pictured anything going wrong.

"I'm the dad," he said. "I'm supposed to think about that."

"All right, so make sure I have enough to get over there and stay safe. Is that all?"

"After. You cannot ignore what happens after. When you come home, I don't want you to be broke."

"I don't think I'm going to be broke, Dad."

"I hope not. But you better have a plan to not be broke."

"Okay, what should I do?"

"Gather information, do your research, figure out how much you will spend every day, and let's go over it."

"When can we do this?" I asked.

"Next week."

This research boosted my confidence about the trip and revealed some important logistics. It forced me to look into the costs and plans that I would not have considered otherwise. We made slow but steady progress with the money details. Then we talked about communication. In terms of money, I had to give in a little bit and abide by Dad's preferences. But in regard to communication, Dad had to adjust.

"You don't know what can happen over there," he began, "so we're going to need to keep in touch."

"I didn't think about that, but you're right," I conceded.

"We'll to talk to you every day, or at least every other day."

"What?" I shouted. "Why on earth would we need to do that?"

"We have to know where you are and that you're safe!" he insisted.

With crystal clear conviction, I said, "Dad, that's the romance of this trip. I want to get lost!"

For a few moments, we just looked at each other. I broke the silence.

"It's fine if you want to talk, and I do want to keep in touch. I just don't see making the effort to get to a phone to talk to you every day. This is my trip."

Dad thought for a second, then asked, "When do you want to talk?"

"I don't know," I said. "Let's just say once a week, then see what happens when I get there."

This seemed to be a good compromise. We had found a middle ground and continued forward.

In the weeks and months before I left, our sessions prepared both of us for my departure. I addressed most of Dad's concerns, and his insistence on and attention to the details helped me plan a phenomenal trip. Now when we think back and talk about those sessions, we laugh about our weighty disagreements and concerns. Like most events, they seemed cataclysmic in the moment, but lost their significance over time. On more than one occasion, my dad has talked about a particular flash point that I had forgotten entirely, and vice versa.

We each learned lessons from that experience, but the main thing was that we opened up and tried to see things from the other person's point of view. Instead of damaging our relationship, we improved it by establishing a respectful partnership. The results were incredible. We are both proud of how we worked through what could have ended up in bitter resentments, and that process of preparing and communicating has helped me plan every ambitious endeavor since then. By looking at things from my dad's perspective, I learned to map out a budget and evaluate the best way to make it happen, and I've followed that practice ever since.

Fans of *Lord of the Rings* lost their minds when the film was released in the early 2000s. I hadn't read the books, but knew that these epic films would mean a great deal to a lot of people. When a friend and I were discussing how he should ask a girl he liked for a date, I told him to just call her up and ask her out. He quoted the movie.

"One does not simply walk into Mordor," he responded in his best impression of Gandalf, one of the major characters.

"I have no idea what you just said."

"It means that it's not as simple as it seems," he said.

"What are you talking about?"

"It's one of the most famous lines from *Lord of the Rings.*"

"Haven't seen it," I said.

"What???!!! How do you function as a human being?"

Here's my pet peeve: When someone asks me if I've seen a movie, and I tell them I haven't, they act like I'm from another planet. That never feels good. I hate being judged for stuff like that. Is there some master list of movies that all earthlings must see?

Because of my strong feelings about this, I try to be extra careful about how I react to people whose experiences are different from mine. If someone hasn't seen a movie, played a sport, visited a tourist attraction, or had some other life experience that seems like a given in my world, I don't ever want to put them down.

> The sooner we can be at peace with the fact that our lives don't have to look like our parents' lives, the easier it is to let go of any obligations we feel to pursue the parent-prescribed path.

That's a great attitude to take with your parents, too. Their life and upbringing is extremely different from yours. Rather than get hot and bothered about it, we need to accept that our parents are, besides being our family, fellow human beings. We know them, but we don't know everything about them, which includes their histories. Just as their past might not look like ours, our future may not match what they envision. The sooner we can be at peace with the fact that our lives don't have to look like our parents' lives, the easier it is to let go of any obligations we feel to pursue the parent-prescribed path.

Thanks for reading "Permission to Play"!!! We greatly appreciate your support!

What's next?

Here's some ideas:

--Post a review on Amazon.

Never done it? It's easy. Get on Amazon, find Permission to Play by Joe Fingerhut, click on "Write a review," and type away. Feel free to enter 5 stars, or whatever ranking you feel it deserves. Make it as short or long as possible. For example, you could put: "This book is the greatest book in history, and every human on the planet should read it." Or something simpler.

--Share it on your page! #permissiontoplay

You are cool. People like you. People like what you like. So let them know you like "Permission to Play." Post the Amazon link on Facebook, Twitter, Instagram, LinkedIn, and whatever other channel you love. Let people know you have it, love it, and how they can benefit from it.

--Help Joe connect with your audience.

Joe speaks at schools, conferences, and companies across America and around the world. And he'll bring books with him. Are you planning an event at your school, office, or organization, or do you know someone who is? Put us in touch with them, and let's set the stage on fire together!

Because my dad didn't support my initial European ambitions, I thought he was stubborn, unfair, and didn't want me to have any fun. I thought his effort to steer me away from this dream was like setting a curfew in high school and that he thought this unreasonable display of power would do some good. I had a lot of resentment about it, just like I did with my adolescent curfew. At the same time, I was afraid that without my parents' support, any hope of this journey would evaporate.

I was in quite a funk. I was determined to succeed and could feel myself developing an attitude of opposition toward my parents. I felt like a hockey goalie decked out in full pads but unable to deflect their relentless slap shots. The pressure built as I researched and explored ways to make my trip to Europe happen, knowing that I was going against my parents' wishes.

Several key people helped me work through this stress. My friend Katie, who gave me the book about backpacking and who had told me that you only have five or six friends in life, was a middle child like me. Her parents hadn't traveled much either. We talked about the stress from our parents.

"My parents are totally freaking out about Europe," I told her. "It's stupid. What should I do?"

"Joe, consider their travel history. Where has your family gone?" she asked.

"We've always been a traveling family. They piled all six of us in the minivan every summer, and we took a road trip somewhere."

"Just around Missouri?" she asked.

"We would alternate summers. For one summer, we'd go to a state park in Missouri to camp, canoe, swim, hike, and all that. And we'd always do one big road trip every other summer. When we went to Chicago, it seemed like everyone was wearing Air Jordans. That's when I decided that the White Sox were my second favorite baseball team."

"Where else did you go?"

"We drove to Colorado, all the way up to Pike's Peak, and we also went to Tennessee, Washington, D.C., Texas, and Minnesota. We went to a bunch of places, and I loved traveling. I thought my parents did too."

I could see the light bulb go off in her head.

"Have your parents ever been on an airplane?" she asked.

I sat back, and thought for a bit. "I know Dad went on a work trip once. He flew from St. Louis to Boston. I don't know about Mom. I don't think she has flown much, if at all."

"There you go. They haven't done anything close to what you want to do."

"But shouldn't they be excited for me?" I said.

"Look, my parents are the same way," Katie said. "They haven't had the same experiences—or the same opportunities—that we have. Where did your parents grow up?"

"Dad grew up in south St. Louis city. There were five kids, and they lived in a two-bedroom apartment. My grandpa had a bunch of jobs. I remember he was a driver for a company president, then he spent a bunch of years with a phone company."

"What about your mom?"

"Mom was raised in Iowa, then they moved to Illinois. She was the oldest of three, and her dad sold insurance. Both of my grandmas stayed home to raise the kids, while both grandpas worked their whole lives."

"Big families, dads worked, moms raised the kids," she said.

"Exactly."

"Did your parents raise you like your grandparents raised them?" she asked.

"Pretty much. My family wasn't poor, but I always felt like other people had it much better than we did. Mom and Dad were always so strict about spending and were focused on how to work hard and save money. My older sister started babysitting in junior high, and I started mowing lawns as soon as I was strong enough to handle the lawnmower on my own," I said.

"So your parents probably don't believe in taking a few months off to find yourself, let alone doing it on another continent. Maybe you should think about that."

There it was. My parents were strongly opposed to my plan to go to Europe because my goals were way beyond the scope of their own experiences.

After that, I stopped fighting my parents on every point and focused on why they felt the way they did. I saw that I needed to give them any and all information they needed to feel informed and more assured that I would be okay. This was new territory for all of us, and we had to discover the path together. It wasn't easy at first, but once our lines of communication opened up, we worked through it and came out stronger.

My backpacking adventure also gave Mom and Dad a taste for what was to come. Years later, my siblings followed suit and also explored other countries, and my sister studied in Mexico City for a semester. We even convinced our parents to go visit her. Instead of refusing to take an international trip, they had learned from my experiences to open their minds to new possibilities. They flew to Mexico, spent a week there, and loved it.

Communicating with your parents about your dreams and expectations can exhaust even the most well-intentioned person. I found that the best way to deal with my parents was to take action and find my own way.

> I found that the best way to deal with my parents was to take action and find my own way.

No matter what, the one thing that most parents want for their children (other than good health) is for them to be happy, and to be happy, we have to find our own way. We can amass all kinds of advice and strategies and can gather insights from experts, teachers, friends, and strangers, but if we don't take action, we'll stagnate and end up in a confused and unfulfilled place. We have to see what works for us and what does not fit. Taking action brings us closer to that elusive state of happiness.

The paths we take and the choices we make might not always be perfect, but the best part of finding our own way and making our own decisions is that we will never have to second-guess ourselves for why we did what we did. We made that choice because it felt true. But if you make choices because someone else is pressuring you to do it their way, you can end up with a lot of regret. And regret opens the door to resentment, which creates a lot of emotional baggage. When you decide your own course and choose to live with the consequences, you and you alone are responsible for the results. The scary part is that you have to take full responsibility, even if the results aren't what you thought they would be. But when everything works out well, you get to take the credit!

Other people's expectations

My cousin, David, is ten years older than me and seemed to have life figured out. During my last few months of college, we became as close as brothers. David didn't have a wife or kids yet, but seemed to have everything else together. I was struggling with what I would do next and asked his advice.

"How did you handle your dad's expectations regarding work?" I asked him.

"There's no easy answer, Joe," he said. "I didn't know what I wanted to do, but I knew I had to get a job to pay my bills. I tried a couple of different jobs, mainly in sales and marketing, and gradually got into financial planning. My dad's happy about it now."

"What do you like about your life?" I asked.

"Business is good. I get to help people. I have my own house, a nice car. I feel pretty lucky."

David seemed to have a lot of freedom, and most importantly, he had built his own life. I loved numbers, money, and people, and it seemed like his career involved all three. It seemed like being a financial planner would be a decent way to spend my working years.

But the idea of managing money didn't make my heart soar. I could picture myself in David's position, but couldn't picture myself in love with it—the word "job" came to mind. A career as a financial planner seemed interesting and profitable, but it still ranked up there with the other conventional options.

Then I played darts with Sara. We had known each other for about eight years, and in our group of friends, she was the 'odd bird.' Tall but not towering, pretty but not gorgeous, Sara stood out for her smile and positive energy. She spontaneously danced at random times, and we all accepted that she had music in her heart. I don't remember having many serious conversations with Sara, but one night when we were celebrating a friend's birthday at a restaurant, we decided to play darts in the game room.

"So, Joe, what do you want to do with your life?" she asked.

"I think I might want to work with people's money," I said, with a slight nod, as if to convince myself of its truth.

"No," she said firmly. This girl, the happy crazy-girl who danced to her own music, turned dark and serious. Her eyes locked with mine, her smile vanished, and her eyebrows creased.

"You will NOT do that," she declared.

"Why not?"

She was firm and serious. "You are capable of SO MUCH MORE than that, Joe."

"Okay, so what should I do?"

"I don't know," she said." But not THAT."

I laughed to hide my discomfort, and I don't think Sara ever knew how much that exchange meant to me.

After that, whenever I had to make a significant decision about a job or life experience, I flashed back to that night. Sara had been a friend, but she had never been my closest friend. But she knew me, and I felt bound to live up to the potential she saw in me. I wanted to fulfill the expectations she had for me. In short, I didn't want to sell out.

EXCUSE BUSTER:

Try a new approach! Identify your desires, share them with your parents, don't worry about getting their approval at first, and ask them about their experiences.

Ask:

1. When have your parents disagreed with you about something you wanted to do?
2. How did you handle that?
3. What was the outcome?
4. In the end, did they ultimately agree or disagree with you?
5. Could you see and appreciate their point of view?
6. What steps did you take to consider things from their perspective?
7. Do you feel like they tried to see things from your perspective?
8. How much do you know about your parents' history?
9. What jobs have they had?

10. How did they meet?
11. Why did they make the particular decisions they made about school, job, spouse, etc?
12. Name some things that you want to do that is NOT on your parents' list of life experiences.
13. How are your parents' expectations, or even your own beliefs, holding you back?

Act:

1. Initiate a conversation with one or both of your parents. Start with, "What was life like for you at my age?"

Excuse 3

I Don't Have Enough Money

This planet has — or rather had — a problem, which was this: Most of the people living on it were unhappy for pretty much all of the time. Many solutions were suggested for this problem, but most of these were largely concerned with the movement of small green pieces of paper, which was odd because on the whole it wasn't the small green pieces of paper that were unhappy.
                    from "The Hitchhiker's Guide to the Galaxy"

Money's only good for the good that it can do.
                                        Marty Domitrovich

As much as money can help you, your attitude about money can also limit your thinking. Money was one of my dad's first objections to my travel in Europe, which is a pretty conventional reaction when faced with an opportunity to pursue a unique interest, skill, or employment opportunity.

"I don't have enough money to do that," you might say.

Even if that's technically correct, it's a mistake to believe it because that belief can prevent you from taking action toward your grandest dreams.

Adding one word makes a difference

Did you know that one single word can have a profound effect on your attitude about money? Whatever you think of your financial situation, you can neutralize that negative inner voice that tells you that you can't do it. Your entire perspective can be changed by adding one word: *Yet*.

Instead of saying, "I don't have the money to do that," add that one little word.

"I don't have the money to do that *yet*."

This simple three-letter word can reprogram your mind and completely alter your mindset. It turns things positive and keeps your hopes alive. This one word can convert a bleak perspective to a long-term vision with potential for pretty big success. Add the word *yet* to your vocabulary and use it often!

When problems are temporary, solutions often lie nearby. Money is a temporary problem, which means there are always solutions. The solutions may not be easy to discover or implement, but they do exist! It is your job to find them.

Travel is actually affordable

Travel in our family meant road trips in the mini-van with Dad, Mom, my two sisters, and brother. Our cheap approach to these trips told me that it was all we could afford. Whenever my friends talked about their trips to Florida or California, I repeated the mantra of my parents: We don't have enough money. When I heard the word *vacation*, I envisioned luxurious hotels, five-star resorts, expensive restaurants, and high price tags. I assumed that only rich people could travel and that the gigantic boulder of money blocked the path of middle-class families like mine.

When a group of my friends studied abroad in Rome, I naturally thought I couldn't afford it. Those same boulders blocked my path. But my European adventure chipped those boulders into smaller rocks that could be removed with ease.

Conserving my money was a priority, regardless of where I traveled. My first night in Paris began at The Blue Planet, a hostel recommended in a backpacker publication.

"Can you believe this hostel is ten bucks a night?" the girl next to me asked. She sat down on a used but comfortable couch in the common area next to the lobby.

"Yeah, this is pretty amazing," I said. "Have you stayed at a lot of these?"

"Only a few so far. I'm not here very long. But this is the nicest one yet."

"You sound American. Where are you from?" I asked.

"California. I'm studying abroad in Spain, but my friends and I are in Paris for the weekend. How about you?"

"I'm from St. Louis, just traveling for a few months. This is my first hostel, first night in Europe."

"Wow, a few months? You must be rich!" she said.

"Far from it. Just trying to see if this whole backpacking thing works."

"But how are you paying for this?" she asked.

"The books I read and the people I talked to made it sound like I could do it without spending a bunch of money," I said.

"It's great," she said. "You will love it! We're just students, but we've gone to a bunch of different cities."

"Tell me what you've done, and let me in on your travel tips," I said.

A big smile lit up her face, and she shared her experiences with a giddy listener.

"Two things," she said. "Sleep on the trains, and get food at grocery stores."

"Okay, but isn't that weird, sleeping on trains?" I asked.

"No, they have sleeping cars and benches that turn into beds. When you do that, you combine your transportation with your accommodation, and the trains are pretty cheap."

"Sweet!" I said. "I have a Eurail pass, so I'm looking forward to using it. Tell me about grocery stores. Easy to find? Crazy food inside?"

"Actually, the stores are everywhere," she said, "just like in America. It could be a small market or a fruit stand or a bigger grocery store. Never anything crazy like the huge stores at home, but you can always find what you need."

"Like what?" I asked. "I'm not quite a shopping expert."

"Anything you need. Food is food. Pick up some meats, cheeses, bread, and you got yourself some sandwiches. Bottled water, drinks, snacks, whatever. The package might have a different language on it, but you'll know what food to get."

"This helps so much! Now what about going to monuments or museums and stuff?"

"You have to pick and choose. You can't do everything," she said.

"So what do you do?" I asked.

"Depends on what you like and what you can afford. You don't need to go to every single museum in the city and pay admission, unless you are totally into art and have a bunch of money," she said.

"So don't go to museums?" I asked.

"No, only go to ones that you want to. If you don't want to go or don't have the money, just wander around the city. We're in Paris, and we're from America. This whole city is like a museum! It's free to walk around."

I found a grocery store where I bought food for my explorations on foot. I had no need or desire to eat every meal in a restaurant. My restaurants were park benches with gourmet layouts of ham and cheese sandwiches with cookies for dessert, and it cost less than five dollars. Occasionally I would join new friends at a restaurant for dinner, and on those occasions, what I saved on grocery store meals allowed me to enjoy their company and the food guilt-free.

In Paris, I learned that I didn't have to say "yes" to everything. I never made it into the top of the Eiffel Tower, mainly because the tickets were so expensive. Instead, the magnificent view from the Arc de Triomphe provided a less expensive panorama that included the Eiffel Tower.

On numerous occasions, I did exactly what that girl had suggested. I combined my transportation with my accommodations to save on costs. I traveled between cities at night to avoid the cost of a hotel. Every once in a while, the surface where I slept was pretty uncomfortable, but I always got to my destination city.

I figured out a way to make it through. At first I didn't think I would have enough money, but I took action, researched my options, and kept an open mind, which, when combined, reduced that money problem to rubble.

Put money issues aside

When Michiyo and I began to plan our honeymoon, we had to consider our finances. We both had experience traveling sensibly, or in other words, on the cheap. Some think that a proper honeymoon must be at an all-inclusive resort in the Caribbean or other exotic locale that carries a price tag of several thousand dollars. That did nothing for us; we wanted to get the most bang for our buck. I didn't mind a serious investment in our honeymoon, but I wanted it to have the highest value.

Using my Europe experience as a model, we banished all limiting thoughts about money and started our research. Our goal was to go somewhere neither of us had been before that had romantic appeal—and not go broke doing it.

At some point, jumping into the craziness of Carnivale in Rio de Janeiro entered my head. The Brazilians specialize in this world-renowned celebration of Mardi Gras. I had seen pictures and video of throngs of people in parades and at parties, wearing the most outlandish costumes imaginable. Going to Carnivale seemed like a great way to kick off a trip across South America.

Of course, that small voice inside my head warned me that this crazy idea would be way out of our price range, but I did my best to ignore it. The crazier the logistics seemed, the more I wanted to do it. Why couldn't two newlyweds backpack across South America for two months?

As we started our research, we warmed to the idea. Truth be told, once I put the issue of money aside, the details came together in a hurry. Various resources such as blogs, magazines, online connections, and friends who had lived in or visited South America confirmed that we could backpack like I had in Europe. If we could deal with hostels, busses and trains, and avoid the high-end options of dining and transportation, the main expense would be our flight. The outlandish idea of a cross-continental adventure in South America seemed within our reach.

Michiyo loved the idea, which affirmed that she would be not only the perfect companion for travel, but the perfect

> Truth be told, once I put the issue of money aside, the details came together in a hurry.

companion for life in general. We bought our tickets and traveled coast-to-coast in South America for two months, from Rio de Janeiro, Brazil, to Lima, Peru. In between, we took busses, trains, and one plane across five countries: Brazil, Argentina, Uruguay, Bolivia, and Peru. What some people would have spent in just one week, we stretched out over two months to put together a lifetime of memories. And we had just begun.

At the end of our honeymoon, I took some time to reflect. The five-year period from my senior year of college until then had included travel to almost two dozen countries, and I was as far from rich as St. Louis is from Tokyo. I'd put together a trip through Europe, a three-year adventure in Asia, and an epic two-month honeymoon in South America. Money was anything but a roadblock to the things in life that excited me.

On our plane ride home from Peru, I was determined not to take this momentum for granted, so I took out a notebook and wrote down my thoughts. What could we do next?

I wrote down *Around the World Trip. How much?*

I considered how much income we would lose and how much we needed to pay bills while we were gone. On that flight, my next idea hatched: We would take an around-the-world trip and end it by spending a month at Michiyo's family's home in Japan. The details weren't clear just yet, but I knew it could be done, and I went to work.

Construct a budget

If you think, "I don't have enough money to do something," it may mean that you either don't have a budget, or you have a budget but haven't taken any action based on it. A budget is nothing but a plan for your income and expenses within a defined amount of time. That plan is not always easy to make, but with some effort you can make it simple. Don't be put off by the grown up stuff here. It's part of figuring out how to live a life of your dreams, and it's well worth it.

A good place to start is by looking at your bills, such as rent, car insurance, health insurance, cell phone, tuition, student loans, groceries, and whatever else. Then you can focus on your debts, which include unpaid bills and anything you owe to friends or relatives. When all that is accounted for, you can address your income.

Just like writing lists, making a budget can reduce the clutter and chaos inside your brain. Bills and debts become stressful when they are not inventoried. My moments of highest stress have come from trying to juggle too many obligations at one time. When I formed a budget, those concerns became less intense. Any time you can make a list of every detail of your financial life, you take that chaos out of your head, put it on paper, and free that space in your mind to go solve the problem. What a benefit!

My dad taught me about budgeting. When he finally realized that I was going to Europe no matter what, he wanted to make sure I had all my bases covered.

"You cannot run out of money in the middle of your trip," he said.

"I know, you told me." I rolled my eyes.

"And you can't come home and have nothing left," he said.

"Dad, you already said that, too. What do you want me to do?" I asked.

"Make a budget."

"Make a budget? What does that even mean? I've never done anything like that before," I said.

"You have some money from your summer jobs. Figure out how much that is. Then figure out how much you're going to spend there," he said.

"But I don't know how much I need, so how can I do that?" I said.

Dad went into math teacher mode, like he was giving instruction in word problems.

"You have to buy a plane ticket," he explained. "And you know your beginning and end dates. Then estimate how much you will spend every day."

"So, figure out how much I'll spend every day, even though I don't know exactly what I'll be doing?" I asked.

He broke it down further.

"Make a list of what your totals would be if you spent fifty dollars a day, thirty dollars a day, and twenty dollars a day. Then see how that compares to the money you already have."

Once he put it in those terms, I wasn't that intimidated. I put pen to paper and had a calculator next to me just to confirm the totals. I started with the round number of two months, which would be sixty days.

Amount	# Days	Total
$50.00	60	$3,000.00
$30.00	60	$1,800.00
$20.00	60	$1,200.00

I took it to Dad. "You don't have $3,000," Dad said.

"From what I have read, I won't need to spend fifty dollars a day," I told him.

"What about your plane ticket?" he asked.

"Don't know yet, but in the $500-700 range," I said.

"Any left over money?" he asked.

"With the money I saved up from working the last couple of summers, I have a little less than $3,000. I think I'll have a few hundred bucks left over when I come back," I said.

Dad looked at my numbers again. It was clear that he still wasn't comfortable about me going to Europe by myself, and he had done his best to throw the money obstacle in my way—and I had addressed it.

"Okay," he said. "Looks like you're covered. Let's keep talking about everything else."

I left the room and smiled. I had scored one victory for that day.

After the first week in Europe, I knew that everything would be okay in terms of money. Even in Paris, which I figured would be one of the most expensive cities, the prices were lower than expected on most things. Hostels cost around ten dollars a night, and I bought the essentials for meals at grocery stores, which saved a bunch on food expenses. And I resisted the urge to do every single tourist thing, which would have emptied my pockets in a hurry.

In Europe, I learned an important life lesson about how to make money fit my life, as opposed to making my life fit around money. I realized that life in general could be full of rich experiences without name-brand, top-of-the-line stuff.

As my habits became stronger and my knowledge grew deeper, I came to believe that a brand new fancy car would give me less money to spend on other things. The same was true of clothes, electronics, furniture, and almost anything you can spend money on. My opinion about how I spend money is the only one that matters, and I spend my money based on the budget I create.

Make a plan with that budget

If Europe felt like a dream, coming home to America was like an alarm clock that jarred me from a deep sleep. So many mornings I wanted to go back to sleep and return to that dream, but I couldn't do that. I had enough money to get by for a little while, but ultimately, I had to find a job.

My heart screamed to make decisions based on my passion, but my mind won out, and I gravitated toward conventional income. My knowledge, experience, and confidence did not yet support going after something that wasn't "normal." I settled into a management position with Cutco, where I had worked for several summers. They helped me open my own office in Kansas City.

We hired and trained students who worked in the summer, and spent lots of money on things like newspaper ads and supplies that could and should have produced revenue sooner than later. Like any business run by a rookie, I had a lot to learn and made many mistakes. At the end of that first summer, our office broke even, which meant that our revenue barely exceeded our expenses. I had little money and even less happiness; it was a bad combination. My future seemed bleaker every day.

At the end of August, the bills arrived for the services we'd used since the beginning of summer. I had no prior business experience, and this cycle of income versus bills was a steep learning curve. I moved into an apartment with another manager who was taking a few months to tie up loose ends, so he could get out of the business. He had organized and paid for all our advertisements at the beginning of the summer, and I owed him several thousand dollars, in addition to rent for every month. Between those bills, student loan payments, car payments, and other expenses, I figured that I needed $10,000 over the next few months to get back on my feet. I felt trapped. The road ahead would be long, and I had no map to proceed.

Fortunately, my roommate and I became close friends, although our friendship did not mean that he forgave my debts. As the classic saying goes, my good friend Duane didn't give me fish to eat for that day; he taught me to fish, so I could eat for the rest of my life.

Duane was diplomatic but firm. "Joe, here's the bill for our advertising," he said. He handed me a slip of paper that showed that my share was $4,000.

"This is what I owe you?" I asked. "How come I didn't know about this?"

"Sorry, man, this is what we agreed to at the beginning of the summer," he said.

I just stared at it.

"Can you pay this?" Duane asked.

"This may as well be a million dollars," I said in an apologetic tone. "I don't have anything close to that."

"I don't need it all now," he said. "But this is too much money to just let things float and eventually forget."

"Definitely," I agreed, even though I secretly wished he would do just that.

"So what do you want to do?" he asked.

"Let me give you something at the end of this month," I said, "and then go from there."

Duane was fine with that, and we didn't talk about the money again for a few weeks. Toward the end of the month, Duane approached me.

"It's the end of the month," he began. "How much can you pay right now?"

My only focus had been to pay the minimum amount for my other bills that month. My debt to Duane never left my mind, but I had done nothing to save for it, much less pay him anything. I felt horrible, but there was nothing I could do at that moment. So I was honest with him.

"I don't have much to pay you," I said.

Duane took a breath and exhaled. "Did you save anything?" he asked.

"I thought I would have extra, but I don't," I said.

He nodded and considered how to handle this dilemma. I owed him a lot of money. Lucky for me, Duane is a very even-keeled guy.

"Joe, have you ever made a budget?" he asked, with no trace of anger or impatience.

My face lit up. "Yes!" I said. "For Europe! My Dad made me do it. I made a list of what I would spend every day to make sure I could afford it."

"That's good, but this is different. We need to figure out how much all of your bills are, and how much money you need to make, so you can start saving. Would you like help with that?"

"Absolutely," I said, both relieved and excited to work with Duane on this.

Duane was right. This was different. When I prepared my budget for Europe, I didn't know how much I would need, but this time, my action plan was based on known amounts. Together we mapped out the next four months. We figured out how much I would pay him each month, so I could be free and clear by the end of the year. That was part one.

"Now you need a plan," he said.

"Isn't this enough? We have the budget down on paper," I said.

"A budget is no good if you don't have a plan you can follow to make it happen."

> "A budget is no good if you don't have a plan you can follow to make it happen."

"So what's next? What's the plan?" I asked.

"You're still focused on the management stuff right now, but it doesn't seem like you're making much money at it."

"I'm not, and I don't really like it. I feel like I have to build the business now, so I can make money later. But I don't enjoy it. It doesn't seem like people who are successful at this have any time to enjoy once they do start making money."

"All right," he interrupted. "I'm just gonna say something." He cupped his hands over his mouth like a bullhorn and yelled, "QUIT!" at the top of his lungs.

Duane was right, but I didn't know what to do. My heart was in a backpack in Europe, but I was stuck in a debt-ridden, unhappy life in Kansas City.

"You're right," I said. "What should I do?"

"Do whatever you need to do to get to the next thing. Stop trying to hire people. That's clearly not working, especially if your heart isn't in this. Just focus on sales for the next few months. You know you're good at that. Pay off your debts and get out."

It all made sense. "That's what I'll do. And I AM going to pay you back," I said.

"I hope so," Duane said with a smile.

I was transformed. Having a plan to follow and a budget changed my behavior. I had one single goal: to be clear of all debts by the end of the year.

I listed the various milestones on a white board next to my bed, so I would keep myself on track. Every time I had a decision to make that involved money, that whiteboard popped into my head. I refused weekend trips with friends. I borrowed movies and watched them at home instead of going to a theater. I was completely focused on making the best decisions to reach my budget goals.

Those were challenging months, and every dollar that came in was headed somewhere that wasn't my own bank account. The plan showed me what I needed to do every day to take a step toward the goal. The path never got easier. I did what I had to do, followed my plan, and the only joy I had was when I crossed off one of the milestones on that white board.

My intentional effort to pay off my debts to a good friend made me a person of integrity. And success followed. During that time, I tried not to think about the final destination, but the journey itself. I would never become debt free by the end of the year if I didn't take steps this month, this week, the next day, and really, the next hour. At the end of every month, I gave Duane two checks: one for rent, and one for the business debt.

At the end of the year, we had both planned to move out of the apartment and on to other things. We met to settle up.

"Here it is, the last check," I told Duane with a big smile.

"Well done, Bro," he said. "I have to admit, at the beginning, I was a little worried. I didn't see how you would be able to do this."

"I couldn't have done this without you, Duane. Thank you!" I honestly appreciated what he had taught me.

We shook hands, and just like that, I was debt free.

Conquering that debt had two major benefits. I saw the immense, practical reward of setting a goal, making a plan, and following that plan. But I also became clear about what I truly wanted to do. I never wanted to be in a position of debt again, and with every step I've taken since then, I've always considered the financial aspect of it.

But something even bigger happened. When I conquered that debt, I felt empowered to tackle the big picture of my life and to pursue what I wanted to do. My heart and mind were now aligned toward a single purpose: to improve my life. Duane helped me envision a better future that didn't include sales management. When Erica planted the seed to work in Asia, my next step became crystal clear. And when I took control of my financial life, I was empowered to improve in all other areas.

EXCUSE BUSTER:

Get real about money! Analyze how much you have, how much you spend, and how much you save, then make a plan to go after what you want.

Ask:

1. Think about your approach to pursuing opportunities and achieving goals. What are your negative or limiting thoughts?
2. Is there something you'd do if money weren't an issue? What is it?

Act:

1. Make a list of the fixed expenses in your life, if you have any.
2. Make a list of your fixed revenue (wages, other income).
3. Write down ways you can reduce your expenses.
4. Pick one crazy idea that you think is out of your financial league. Write it down as if it is already happening. For example, "I am studying abroad this summer," "I am attending Yale University next year," or "I have an internship in New York City this semester."
5. How much would that cost? Write it down. If you don't know, research it to come up with a loose figure.
6. How long will it take to make that idea a reality?
7. What are three changes you can make right now (either in spending habits, job position, the company you keep, etc.) that would reduce that amount of time? Pick one of them and start doing it NOW.
8. For one day, add the word YET to every sentence when you talk about the things you lack.

Excuse 4

This Isn't The Right Time

If you want to pursue the thing that sets your heart on fire, you may feel stuck because it's so different from what your life is like now. NEWS FLASH: Your current path is not set in stone! Even if your current direction was mandated by someone else, you can adjust your course and make changes. Just put your head down and push forward.

As students, school plays a huge role in how we spend our time, and there's a particular cycle we follow. In America, school starts in the fall and ends in late spring, and we have breaks around the holidays and in the spring. During those breaks, you may strike a pleasant balance between fun, work, and preparation for the next school cycle. But when your school years are over, work will dictate your schedule. Life brings far greater responsibilities and much bigger bills, with far fewer breaks. The work cycle seems longer, and once it begins, it can feel like it will never end. But that's only an illusion.

If you think you can't make changes to your life because you are already committed to a particular cycle, you are cheating yourself. This "set in concrete" mindset can prevent you from pursuing opportunities that fulfill you and make you happy.

Look back from the future

In his best-selling book, *The Da Vinci Code,* Dan Brown's characters faced unrelenting life-threatening situations. The heroine of the story offered me a perspective that I've used for years. She was locked in a small container, but rather than panic, she relaxed her mind. She visualized her future self and created a scene where she reflected back on how she escaped that conundrum, and she used that method to get out. Interesting method!

It's hard to create change when you're looking forward. When the present is uncertain or feels uncomfortable, it creates anxiety that prevents you from finding creative ways to make things better. On the other hand, when you view your present circumstances from a future perspective—like the character in *The DaVinci Code*—things become much more clear.

You know what? Most things don't change that much from month to month and year to year because life has a rhythm composed of cycles. Every winter, the Super Bowl draws people together for a celebration of sport, culture, and funny commercials. It's the same thing every year, just different teams. And then there's baseball. I've been a St. Louis Cardinals fan since birth, and they operate like a clock. Pitchers and catchers report to spring training in February, play pre-season games in March, and Opening Day is in April. The All-Star game is in July, and the World Series is in October. When it's over, there's a stretch of several months without baseball. But that gap is filled by hockey, football, and basketball until we come together with family and friends again for one of the biggest parties of the year: the Super Bowl!

This cycle never ends.

Even if you're not a sports fan, whatever involves you most likely has a similar cycle. Wash, rinse, repeat.

Memorable events, of course, occur during these cycles, and every generation has their *"Where were you?"* moment. Pearl Harbor in the forties, the Kennedy assassination in the sixties, the Challenger explosion in the eighties, the 9/11 attacks in 2001. Significant personal events also create change. You move away from home. You start a new job. You begin a serious relationship—marriage, kids, you buy a house. And ultimately, retirement.

Over the course of a few decades, those are significant changes, but since the typical life span is about seventy-five years, the changes average out to about one every ten years. But we don't really live life in averages, do we? Most of those changes, such as moving away from home, getting into a serious relationship, getting married, and having kids, happen during the period you're in now, between your late teens and early thirties.

Beyond these milestone events, the cyclical nature of life can make it feel like the months and years run together. How you deal with this repetition can have a powerful effect on your choices and your life path. If you think life is repetitive and boring, it's easy to become cynical and think that what you do doesn't matter.

And yet, you can avoid that attitude altogether. If you step back and realize that, just like annual events such as the Super Bowl, incredible opportunities are available to you, too. The timing might not be as predictable, but the cyclical nature of life assures you that, as long as you are open to them, great experiences will find you. If you believe that you, too, will have such opportunities, you can pursue the things that set your heart on fire. In other words, things like school, work, bills, and sports, will always be there, so why not go after an experience that becomes your own personal, generation-defining event?

In other words, things like school, work, bills, and sports, will always be there, so why not go after an experience that becomes your own personal, generation-defining event?

Different paths yield different results

My friend, John, had gone to high school with me, and we were both at Loyola now. We had an interesting conversation right before we started our senior year of college.

"Something doesn't add up," I said.

"Are you talking about math homework?" John cracked.

"No. All this life stuff."

"What do you mean by *life stuff*?" he asked.

"Senior year starts soon. Life happens after graduation, and it doesn't sound like any fun. I like school and all the good things that come with it: fun, friends, learning, challenges."

"Me, too. So what's the problem?"

"I don't feel like I am living life to the fullest," I said.

"That sounds cheesy. You're doing fine," he said.

"I feel that the world offers more, and I'm missing it. There's more to see, and I'm not even trying," I said.

"I recently heard a quote," he said. "Maybe it will help. 'If you want something you've never had, you have to do something you've never done.' I have no idea who said it."

"Exactly," I said. "I've got to do something different."

And I did. I did something I'd never done: I quit the routine. I broke out of the cycle that dictated what I had to do and when I had to do it. I decided that after graduation, I would leave the country for ten weeks, and neither school nor employment would be my focus.

Dad was worried that if I travelled for a few months, when I came back, all the jobs would have been taken by other recent graduates. I reasoned that not much would change from the time I left until the time I returned in December. Businesses would still need employees, and plenty of people would be looking for jobs. Ten weeks would not make or break my life.

So I went, and that experience not only gave me a blueprint for making decisions about my future, but it also gave me the confidence to say "yes" to adventure when others might think their way out of it. I knew that life wouldn't change all that much, and if things didn't work out after Europe, I could always go back to the way I had lived for so long.

When I came back to St. Louis, I found that I had plenty of opportunities to apply my Europe approach. I would say "yes" to something, focus on the challenge of getting there, then worry about how to get home later. Like when I caught up with John to share my pictures and stories with him.

"This is amazing," John said, as he flipped through my photos. "What's next?"

"No idea yet," I said, and that was the truth. "When do you go back to Baltimore?"

John was in the middle of volunteer commitment and was doing service work for a year. He lived in a house with four women, one of whom would become his wife. "I'll start driving back from St. Louis right before New Year's Eve. I have to be back in Baltimore on January 2," he said.

A light bulb went off. "Will you be driving through New York?" I asked.

"Yeah, I'll probably get close to there on the way home," he said.

"What if I ride back with you, and we go to Times Square on New Year's Eve!" I practically shouted.

John thought for a moment. "Do you have time? I mean, don't you have other things to do?"

"I just got back from Europe. Nothing is going on yet. I've always wanted to go to Times Square on New Year's Eve. This is a great chance!" I said.

"You can ride with me, no problem," he said. "But how will you get back home?"

"I have no idea, and that's one more thing that will make it fun. Maybe I can find someone who's driving to St. Louis. Or I could take a bus. I'm not sure," I said.

"Then let's go to New York!" John said.

A few days later we were driving a mini-van across the Midwest on our way to New York. Believe it or not, we had no cell phones or social media at the time, and we had a great time catching up on the last couple of months and reminiscing about our high school friends and memories. After the long drive, we parked the car at a friend's house in New Jersey and took a few trains to the stop that was closest to Times Square. We climbed the steps out of the subway and took it all in.

"I feel so small," John said, as he gazed at the vast expanse of skyscrapers, office buildings, apartments, and everything New York had to offer.

We followed the path through police barricades and down the side streets and ended up in a sea of people. We later learned that an estimated TWO million people were there with us, including a group of about twenty people who stood near us. The group included college kids, married couples, middle-aged parents with kids at home, and some foreign exchange students from Australia and Korea. Large screens were set up on each street corner that showed the countdown to midnight from other cities around the world. As the day went on, the celebrations got louder, until the clock ticked down to midnight.

All of our new friends and plenty of strangers put their arms around each other and, together, we counted down the last seconds. The ball dropped, and a roar exploded from the crowd, locked in at full volume for an entire hour. We took pictures, exchanged contact information, and said our goodbyes.

John and I had managed to find another friend we knew from St. Louis, and he let us crash in his apartment that night. We woke up early the next day because John needed to get back to Baltimore.

"What about you?" he asked. "How are you going to get home?"

"I need to think about it," I said. "I asked everyone last night if they knew any road-trippers who were driving back through St. Louis, but nobody did."

"Or they didn't want to ride with you!" John joked.

"Let's just go to Baltimore, and we'll see what happens," I said.

I thought long and hard about how I would get home. I didn't have a lot of money left. The New Year's celebration in New York had capped off several incredible months in Europe. But it was time for me to get back.

"Drop me off at the Baltimore airport," I told John. "I'll fly home."

After my return from Europe and New York, I told everyone my stories and showed them the pictures. Then came the questions. "What are you going do next? Where will you work? How will you pay your bills?"

The funny thing is that even if I hadn't gone to Europe or New York, they would have asked me these same questions. They just would have come three months earlier. Not much else had changed— except that I got to explore twelve countries on two continents, and I celebrated New Year's Eve in New York City. These were life-changing experiences, and I gained something I never had before: an expanded view of the world. My future self smiled at the choices I had made.

Identify the desired outcome, and work your way backward

In college, I majored in math, not because I wanted to be a teacher, but because I wanted to study something I thought I would enjoy for that four years. I got interested in math in high school, when I spent long hours on complicated equations, proofs, and story problems. I liked to gather information and piece solutions together. And I felt a distinct thrill when I turned to the back of the book and saw that my answers were correct. For the times when my result didn't match the correct answer, I started with the answer and worked my way backwards.

I use that same process to pursue the bigger opportunities in life. I identify the desired outcome and work backward to create a process that will get me there.

If you wanted to take a walk to get some exercise, it wouldn't make much difference if you got tired or thirsty and cut your walk short. You were just out to loosen up and get some fresh air. But if your goal was to hike up a mountain, and you wanted to make it to the top, you'd better have a plan.

My friend, Dave, and his wife hiked to the top of Mount Kilimanjaro in Africa. They didn't arrive in Tanzania and start walking for the exercise; their goal was to get to the summit. So they worked their way backward and prepared for months. They bought the right jackets, pants, tents, shoes, snacks, water containers, and consulted with lots of knowledgeable people about how to do it.

They hiked for days, and when they finally reached the summit, Dave could barely breathe. He was in pain from altitude sickness and was barely able to walk. But with the goal in site, he pushed on and made it to the end, although rather than smile, he grimaced for the memorable photos they took standing next to the summit sign! Dave pushed himself because he could see his target. When the end is in sight, the path, while not always easy, is at least clear.

The plan for Asia

When I decided to move to Asia, I had several goals. I wanted to make and save some money, and I wanted to travel, which led me to the JET Program in Japan. The program gave me a place to live, and as long as I was smart about it, I could save a good bit of my salary. So travel became my key focus.

Traveling during the school term seemed unlikely because when I got my schedule, it was clear that school accounted for eight hours every day. Big disappointment. The work structure I had tried to escape in America was alive and well in Japan. However, this time I had a firm goal in mind. My focus was to explore more of the Asian continent. I knew the what, but didn't know how. So I worked backwards.

My first step was to sit down with one of the veterans from the JET program and ask her to explain my schedule. Tanya had taught in Japan for two years. She went out of her way to provide all of us newbies with information and to answer our questions. She was excited to talk to me about the travel possibilities.

"I have so many questions," I began.

"Tell me what you want to do," Tanya said.

"I want to travel as much as possible this year. Other than weekends, when are the best times to explore?"

"There are two or three main times," she said. "One is during the winter break, and the other is during Golden Week. And you have all summer, too."

"What's Golden Week?"

Tanya smiled. "Golden Week is amazing! At the end of April and beginning of May, a bunch of national holidays are strung together. So you don't have to use a lot of vacation days to put together a solid trip."

I scribbled down all the details.

"And, of course, there's no school during winter and summer breaks, so I'm free to leave, right?" I asked.

"Kind of," Tanya explained. "This is a year-round job, so even when school is not in session, you are expected to be at the Board of Education office."

"So you can still travel if you use your vacation days," I said.

"Exactly. But also, every month seems to have at least one or two national holidays. Some people chunk their vacation days up and take a few big trips, and others take a few days here and there," she said.

"I'm definitely taking a few long trips," I said.

"So here's what you do," she said. "Get your calendar and look at the entire year. Get your school's schedule also, because they might have an extra random holiday or something. Decide when your best times are to go, and then figure out your destinations."

I got to work right away. I focused on two or three major trips outside of Japan, and then made the most of every weekend with local excursions and exploration. I studied the schedule for the entire school year and marked off national holidays—and even found a few other days when school was out. When I finished, I saw that I had three different ten-day periods over the next twelve months when I could travel, with a handful of other weekends that could be extended for three or four-day trips.

Tanya's advice was the catalyst for making the most of that first year in Japan. We saw each other around town sometimes and caught up again just before winter break.

"How's your travel going?" she asked.

"It's been good so far, and it's about to be incredible," I happily told her.

"Great! Tell me about it."

"In November, I went to Korea with a few people for four days. That was the beginning."

"I love Korea! Did you go to Seoul?" she asked.

"Yes, we spent some time in Seoul, took trains all around the city to different landmarks, tried different Korean food, and hit up the cheap shopping areas," I said.

"Did you get to the DMZ?" Tanya asked. She referred to the demilitarized zone that separated North Korea and South Korea.

"Yes, we got up there, and it was creepy! I tried to take a picture, and a guard who was carrying a machine gun blew a whistle at me."

"Yikes! That never happened to me. So where to next?" she asked.

"Thailand! I'll spend about two weeks there over Christmas break. Have you been there?"

"Yes, it's one of my favorite places. Incredible food, super-nice people, and everything is so cheap," she said.

"That's what I hear. I want to hit the beaches."

"Definitely do that. There's one island where the Leonardo DiCaprio movie *The Beach* was filmed," she said. "You should go there."

"I can't wait! Thanks for helping me lay everything out. I've heard about other teachers who take a day off here or there when they need a break. Even if I don't feel like going to school, I will honor my work days, so I can cherish these amazing trips when the time comes," I said.

"Treat those days like gold," Tanya said.

And I did.

My first trip to Thailand included scuba diving, elephant rides, and an all-night dance party on a beach with twelve thousand people for a full-moon celebration. Even though I promised myself that I wouldn't repeat any destinations during my time in Asia, my friends heard all the good stuff about Thailand and convinced me to go with them a few months later for Golden Week. I already had the time mapped out and simply plugged in the destination.

I renewed my contract for another year and returned home for a few weeks in the summer. Then, using that same travel strategy during my second year, I spent almost two weeks each in Hong Kong, New Zealand, and Vietnam. During my third year, I went to China and took another trip home to America. I became adept at finding gaps in my schedule, and I jumped on opportunities to explore a variety of different regions and cities in Japan on the weekends. At the end of three years, I felt like I had squeezed every ounce out of every opportunity, which had been my goal from the beginning.

When I planned my Europe trip, I told everyone about it in the months before I left. When I got to Japan, I told my supervisors and coworkers about my plans for the entire year so that they were in the loop. In both cases, I set a clear goal that allowed me to work backward and to be intentional and effective with my plans, so I could align everyone who might be affected.

I have been fortunate and have made some pretty big dreams come true. These successes allowed me to repeat my method for thinking big: Begin with the vision of a successful outcome, and the path to that success will make itself known.

Get to the root: Why?

Too often, people don't take action toward their dream because they think they're stuck on their current path, but they don't consider WHY they're on that path at all. They haven't taken the time to think about what's best for themselves.

Our fast-paced society constantly bombards us with phone calls, e-mails, texts, posts, messages, shows, links, and countless other shiny objects that steal our time. You must disconnect from this chaos in order to consider the big picture. People get hung up on a lot of little things that keep them happy for a short time, but find themselves flailing at the big things that have the potential to make them happy for a long time.

Once you figure out what sets your heart on fire, the focused pursuit of those things will become your filter for making decisions about how you spend your time, and those time-stealing distractions can get easier to handle. You'll push aside the stuff that doesn't matter and welcome what will benefit your ultimate goal.

When I realized that I wasn't going to be a star athlete in high school, I got involved in a community service group, and I also joined a teen leadership group. Both groups included kids who had either played sports or casually enjoyed sports, so I heard about other alternatives to athletics that I could try. That's where I heard about a dance class I enrolled in at school. I thought that a physical activity like dance would be fun, and I wanted to try something new.

Our teacher was a tiny, high-spirited woman who had been on stage in St. Louis theater as an actress and dancer. Peggy Quinn displayed relentless optimism in a very uncomfortable, all-boys environment, and we responded so well that the school created a second dance class for those of us who wanted to continue. Miss Quinn covered the basics of dance, including tap, jazz, ballet, and variations of ballroom dancing. A room full of private-school boys wearing khakis and dancing with each other made for an amusing sight. We practiced how to lead and how to follow, and even though the class wasn't a sport, I felt excited and closer to something that made me happy.

Miss Quinn saw how much joy dance brought me, regardless of my lack of talent, and she approached me one day with a firm command.

"You need to get in a play," she told me.

"I can't do that, Miss Quinn," I said meekly.

"Well, you're going to go to an audition, and that's it," she said.

"I don't have time. I have homework."

"You can make time. Everybody has homework, and lots of people do plays."

"I've never been in a play before," I protested.

"That doesn't matter. You can dance! The all-girls high schools need guys, and they would love to have you."

Girls? The twist in my stomach told me to do this, and I gave in.

"All right," I said, "if you say so. What do I do?"

"My former high school is having auditions for *Hello Dolly* next week. Just show up and see what happens." Miss Quinn did not take "no" for an answer.

Her confidence buoyed me on the painful drive to the girls' school across town. I convinced a friend, a fellow former athlete and dance classmate, to go, too. Neither of us had any idea what would happen. We parked, asked for directions to the auditions, and headed to the theater.

A woman with a clipboard greeted us at the door.

"Here for auditions?" she said.

"Yes. Uh, yes, we are here, um, for the auditions," I stammered.

"Sign your name here. Are you dancers, actors, or singers?"

My friend and I looked at each other. We hadn't considered this question.

"Dancers," my friend volunteered.

"Maybe actors, also," I added with a little hope in my voice. If stage time was possible, I might as well try that, too.

We opened the doors and walked into a room the size of a small gymnasium. The stage was on one side.

"This is organized chaos," my friend said. "Check it out: singers on stage, dancers at the far end, and actors at the other end.

"Yeah, but it's 90 percent girls!" I pointed out.

We survived the auditions, only because they needed guys, just like Miss Quinn said. Despite little previous experience, I landed one of the main male roles. As Rudolf, the head waiter at Harmonia Gardens Restaurant, I led an entire stage full of dancers in a song-and-dance combination.

During the next three months, from the audition to the performances and cast parties, I found a way to make time in life for something that made me happy. The amount of homework I had didn't change, but my approach to getting everything done did. Every day, I headed straight to rehearsal, then home for dinner and homework. When I was on stage, I felt an adrenaline rush that was my first real indication of what I wanted in life and how I wanted to spend my time. Because I had this new interest, it was easy to tune out everything else that might take my time away from it.

After that, I was part of the cast of *Oklahoma!* at a different all-girls school. I had discovered new skills that gave me the same positive feelings that sports once did, which helped me understand why I liked sports so much: I loved being in front of people. During games, I loved it when parents, siblings, and classmates cheered me on. On stage, that same applause helped me realize that while sports were fun, I was really happy when I was entertaining people. I discovered this because I had taken the time to figure out my "why." Even if I had failed, I still made the effort to be true to what I wanted.

I tried out for several plays in college but didn't find as much fulfillment there as I did in high school. I tried stand-up comedy but didn't fall in love with the journey required to make things happen. My true love was speaking in front of people, which led me to leadership positions as an RA in the dorms, along with various other jobs I had.

Now I make sure that every endeavor is aligned with what sets my heart on fire: speaking, entertaining, helping, serving. This clarity established my unconventional career path and helped me make time for the right things. It also helped me avoid settling for things that didn't fulfill me but satisfied other people's expectations.

EXCUSE BUSTER:

Get moving! Pick something you want to do and take action toward that.

Ask:

1. Do you feel stuck on your current path?

2. Will your future self be happy if you continue on this path? Why or why not?
3. Is there something you enjoy doing but don't see how it relates to a future career?
4. Develop an end goal. Picture yourself ten years in the future, having achieved that goal. What did you do to make that happen? How did you break the cycle that had you trapped?

Act:

1. Make a list of everything you are involved in and all of your commitments.
2. Mark each entry with either "H" or "W." (H = have to be involved, W = want to be involved)
3. For the H's, write down those reasons why you HAVE to be there.
4. For the W's, write down how these activities may lead you to discover something else.
5. Talk about your end goal with an advisor, a parent, or some other family member or friend who can be your a mentor. Write down two or three steps you can take over the next three or four months that will put you on the path to that goal.
6. This week, tell five people about your goal.

Excuse 5

I'm Too Busy

Let me just say it: EVERYONE IS BUSY. No matter what their location, situation, or age, everyone seems to have too many things to do and too little time. And even if we had more time, we would find more things to fill it. The truth is that most people's "busy-ness" stems from their inability to manage the time they have, or at the very least, their failure to examine what matters most and how to make time for those things.

Take control of your time

I picture the passage of time like water flowing down a river. In St. Louis, one of our signature sights is the mighty Mississippi River. As a child, my family often visited the banks of the Mississippi, located only a few blocks from downtown. I never saw an ocean until my teenage years, so it was the biggest body of water I knew.

The Mississippi is a constant flow of muddy, brown water that carries sticks, debris, barges, and the tug boats that transport those barges. My brother and sisters and I would skip rocks across the river and throw branches in the water, then watch them until they floated out of sight. Mom and Dad stood nearby and made sure the strong current didn't sweep us away. I have been on those banks early in the morning, late at night, and all times in between. The current is always swift. I was always afraid that I would fall in and be dragged away into the unknown.

Time is just like the water that flows down the Mississippi River. We cannot stop it. If you fall in, your best choice is to go with the current, because swimming against the current is too exhausting. When you follow the current, not only can you exert some control over the direction you're going, but you can also use the current to help speed you along.

We cannot swim against the current of time, but we can learn to take control within that current, and with practice, the speed of the current will allow us to take advantage of the flow and capitalize on momentum.

Recognize the benefit of delayed gratification

It's important to know that you probably won't achieve success right away. You won't know how to swim with the current when you first jump in the river, but once you get the hang of it, you will go places faster.

You've heard the Hollywood cliché that "It takes thirty years to become an overnight success." The best approach is to embrace the journey, regardless of how long that journey may be. If you are fixated on a quick resolution to a problem or goal, you risk jumping at the first solution you see. You might get lucky and find the right answer right away, but then again, you might not. The first solution may seem like the best, but it could, in fact, turn out to be harmful to your process.

When I thought about backpacking through Europe, I pictured a sunny afternoon walk near the Eiffel Tower. I figured I would just get my plane ticket and go, and everything would take care of itself. The reality was that planning an ambitious trip like this took quite a bit of research and preparation. I had no idea where to start, and like everyone else, I had a lot of other things on my plate.

Because I was a senior in college, my classes became more important as graduation approached. All my ducks had to be in a row in order for me to graduate. When classes finished, I had planned to open my own Cutco office in the summer, which meant that I needed to prepare for that during the school year. Other non-academic pursuits required my attention, too, from retreats and intramural sports teams, to mascot and residence life events. And of course, my friendships and relationships were priorities.

Planning a grand backpack adventure through a bunch of strange countries seemed like a massive undertaking, but my dad—who remained skeptical of the entire endeavor—helped me in the planning stages. We had regular meetings to discuss the different aspects of the trip, which kept me on track with the small tasks that needed to be done along the way. When I saw that I was making progress in small increments, I became less stressed and more excited about the entire process.

One thing at a time

In the months before my trip, I often thought back to a pivotal evening I had in high school. Everything at school was geared toward preparing us for the hard work ahead in college, and we dreaded Fridays because we had tests in almost every subject. The work I did during the week impacted how I did on the tests.

One day I lugged home my backpack filled with six sets of books—one for each subject.

Dad picked me up after soccer practice, and our family ate dinner together. Around six thirty, I sat at my desk in my room and stared at my homework list.

1. History: Read a full chapter and write answers to the chapter summary questions.
2. Biology: Complete a three-page review of Unit 2, which covered three chapters.
3. Algebra: Complete the odd-numbered integer problems, numbers 1-50.
4. Chinese: Review how to write that week's characters, read a chapter in our textbook, and write ten sentences using that chapter's grammar lesson.
5. Theology: Write a reflection paper involving that week's discussion of Biblical ethics.
6. English: Read chapters six through ten in "Catcher in the Rye," and study the twenty vocabulary words that will be on the Friday test.

I had no idea how to I would get through it all in that one night. The clock marched toward seven o'clock. A long soccer practice had capped a full day of classes, and I was exhausted.

"Want to play outside?" my brother asked. He had no worries as a sixth grader.

"Sorry, buddy," I said. "Nothing would make me happier than playing in the backyard right now, but I have too much homework to do."

"Can't you do it later?" he asked.

I took a deep breath. "I have homework in six subjects, and most of them will take close to an hour, if I'm lucky."

"All right," he said, disappointed.

The history textbook came out first. I plowed through paragraphs, not at all interested in the economic conditions of early American settlers. I read and re-read entire paragraphs.

All I wanted to do was sleep. I thought about putting off the history homework, but then I'd have even more chapters to read the next day. Plus all my other assignments would pile up. Then Friday would arrive, and I would have nothing studied. I'd fail the tests and ruin my grades for the semester. Freshman year was only a few days old, and I had four more years of this!

The tension grew inside me like a small fire. Within minutes, I was in tears. I wanted to be done with this stuff and didn't want to spend the next five hours doing all this homework. I dropped my face to my hands and let the tears flow.

Mom was in the next room. Because I was a fourteen-year-old boy, I tried to keep my tears discreet, but she opened my door softly, stood behind me, and put her hands on my shoulders.

"Let it out," she assured in a whisper, while giving my neck and shoulders a gentle rub.

Her words comforted me, which made me cry a little harder. Now that she was already in the room, I had nothing to hide.

"Whatever is wrong, everything is going to be okay," she said.

I caught my breath, and settled down a bit.

"What's up?" she asked.

"I have so much to do," I began. "Soccer practice got done late, it's almost seven thirty, and I have all this to do."

I pointed to the backpack next to my soccer bag. It overflowed with textbooks, color-coded notebooks, and folders for each subject.

She knelt down on one knee and put her face right next to mine. What she said next gave me the blueprint for every deadline dilemma I would ever face in life.

"Just do one thing at a time," she said. "That's all you can do."

"There is so much!" I said, and pushed back. "I'm too busy!"

"You're right. You are busy, Joe. Just get one thing done. Then put that away, and move on to the next. Don't think about doing all of it, just think about what you're working on."

> "Just do one thing at a time," she said. "That's all you can do."

She stayed a few more moments until my breath returned and my eyes dried.

"You don't have to be perfect on all this. Just do your best and get it done," she said, giving me one last pat on the back.

I nodded. "Thanks Mom," I said, and managed a smile. "One thing at a time."

I buckled down and made gradual progress. I put History aside, since I didn't enjoy it and took out Algebra, which I really liked. Those problems took less than an hour. Chinese and English turned out to be pretty straightforward, and soon I wrapped up the Theology assignment as well. With the end in sight, I grinded through the painful Biology homework in less than forty-five minutes.

I tackled the History textbook last. Rather than wear myself out trying to read every word, I focused on finding the answers to the questions at the end of the chapter. My work wasn't perfect, but I got it all done.

My brother was in bed behind me, fast asleep. Lucky for him, a shared bedroom did not mean shared homework. The alarm clock said it was one o'clock. Sixth graders don't stay up till one, and I looked at him with envy.

I went to bed exhausted that night, but I felt a mixture of pride and happiness as relief washed over me. Many more nights of homework like this loomed on the horizon, but for the moment, I could breathe. My head hit the pillow and my gratitude turned into slumber.

Just like that night of homework, I planned the details of my European trip step by step, one thing at a time. I focused on a handful of destinations and left a lot of time for unplanned exploration. Any time someone told me about their knowledge or experience in Europe, I took the time to absorb what they had to say and wrote down the information that would help. Gradually, my plan took shape, even amid the chaos of my senior year.

Planning this trip became a lesson in time management. I had wanted to get it done right away and for it to be perfect, but I learned that if I wanted to get the most out of it, it would require time and persistent, intentional action. Life rarely offers the thing we desire in its completed form. Whatever we want, we have to work for it, little by little, and maintain forward progress. Most of my future accomplishments proved this to be true.

Make a time budget

To take control of time rather than letting time control you, it's important to understand the value of time. I appreciated numbers early in life and became a math major in college. Of all the complicated concepts we studied, one of the most powerful numbers was never discussed in class: 168.

- A day has twenty-four hours.
- A week has seven days.
- 24 hours x 7 days = 168 hours.
- Each week has 168 hours.
- Each week, we have 168 hours to spend.

You must understand how to plan your week's schedule in order to progress toward your goals. Just like an effective financial budget starts by listing all the known factors, an effective time budget lists all your periods of activity.

Let's look at a snapshot of an average day.

Your Daily Time Budget		
Total Hours		24
Sleep	8	
Breakfast	0.5	
Commute	1	
School/Work	8	
Lunch	0.5	
Dinner	1	
Shower/hygiene	0.5	
Practice/tasks	1	
Homework	1	
	21.5	
Left over hours		2.5

Everyone's day and week looks different. For example, you may spend more than one hour on homework, or you may have two hours of baseball or piano practice. You may take long showers. Either way, this chart is an example of an average day, and look how much time is unaccounted for: less than three hours.

What about the weekend, you ask? Let's take that daily chart and extend it across seven days, which includes Saturday and Sunday.

Your Weekly Time Budget		
Total Hours		168
Sleep	56	
Breakfast	3.5	
Commute	7	
School/Work	40	
Lunch	3.5	
Dinner	7	
Shower/hygiene	3.5	
Practice/tasks	5	
Homework	7	
Part time job	10	
	142.5	
Left over hours	weekly	25.5

This assumes that a part time job takes up ten hours a week, which leaves you less than four hours per day of free time.

Think about that. After you account for all the essentials, you have between two and four hours a day, or fourteen to twenty-eight hours in a week, left to make something of your life. Every day offers a chunk of hours that sit there like money in the bank.

How can you capitalize on that time? Now that you see where the current is taking you and how fast it's going, you can take advantage of that momentum to create magic in your life.

If you have a structured approach to how you spend your time, it provides accountability and helps manage your expectations. If you have a lot to do, but simply assume that everything will get done without having a real plan behind it, your probability of failure is high. But if you lay out a structured schedule beforehand, you are much more likely to be successful. A time budget turns *someday* into *today*, and changes *I thought about doing that* to *I did it!*

> A time budget turns *someday* into *today*, and changes *I thought about doing that* to *I did it!*

Here's your challenge: For one week, use your calendar to keep track of your day in fifteen-minute increments. Write down exactly what you did every fifteen minutes of every day. It sounds like a lot of busy work, and it is, but it's easy to do once you get started. At the end of the week, take a look at what you wrote and think about where you might have used your time better. Doing this is almost guaranteed to change your mind about how valuable your time is and how much you can get done.

EXCUSE BUSTER:

Think you're too busy? Get real about time and use it to your advantage!

Ask:

1. Do you feel bogged down by all the little things you have to do?

2. For your main goal, are you trying to do everything at once? Do you have a plan?

Act:

1. Keep track of your time in fifteen-minute increments for one week. Write it down!
2. At the end of the week, answer these questions: What were you most proud of? Where could you improve?
3. Keep track of time in fifteen-minute increments for one more week. Review your previous week's notes. How did you improve? Which action made the biggest difference, and what will you continue to do moving forward?

Excuse 6

I Don't Have The Experience

One of my neighbors has a yard full of dandelions, and when spring turns into summer, he cuts his grass real short. The next day, hundreds of dandelions sprout. Dandelions are a lot like excuses.

Whether it's that inner voice that tells you that you aren't good enough, or something a family member or friend says that plants the seed of doubt, you can always find an excuse not to do something. Add "I don't have the experience" to that list of excuses. That's what worried my dad when he tried to put the brakes on my trip to Europe.

Even if you don't have experience in the particular thing you want to do, you can learn a lot by doing a little research. When you know your goal, research can help you figure out the path—or at the very least, your first step.

> When you know your goal, research can help you figure out the path—or at the very least, your first step.

Find a way in

My lack of foreign travel experience was a major concern. I wanted to see a lot of different places but had no idea where to start. My first goal was to find a person or an organization that could provide a guiding hand or show me a baby step.

The perfect opportunity presented itself within a few weeks. I was walking to class with a girl who'd been involved in community service for a few years. I told her that I had a plan to visit other countries, and she understood my hesitance because I'd had never traveled like that before.

"You should go on a foreign service trip," she said.

"I have heard about those," I said. "They had them at my high school. I assumed they were too expensive."

"They aren't cheap, but Loyola puts together a great trip. You do a lot of fundraising to help pay for it."

"I thought rich kids went on those trips, and their parents paid for it," I said.

"Some people are in that boat, but most of them are kids who pay a little bit themselves, and raise the rest of the funds," she said.

"So you have to ask family and friends for money?" I asked.

"You can, but there are also programs to help you, like selling raffle tickets at sporting events and to businesses. It's not bad at all," she said.

"But I am not a community service person," I said. "In high school I went to a foster home, and I served food at a soup kitchen, but I haven't done much other than that," I said.

"Great! That's more than what a lot of people have done," she said. "You should apply!"

"Will they help me get a passport?" I asked.

"They walk you through everything," she said. "It's really great for someone like you because you get to go on a trip that is totally planned by the school. You can use everything you learn through that experience when you travel to other countries on your own."

"Do you have to miss school?" I asked.

"No, they schedule the trips over our spring and winter breaks," she said. "Do some research and see if one of these trips would work for you."

Soon after, I went to the Community Service office and found out about the next available trip, a two-week service trip to Guatemala over winter break. I picked up a brochure and talked to the lady at the desk.

"Tell me a little bit about this trip," I said.

"Guatemala is great!" she said. "I went there two years ago, and I would totally go back again."

"How does everything work, like getting a passport and all that?"

"You'll be with a group of about ten students and teachers. There are leaders who have taken this trip before, and they help you get a passport if you don't have one. They also direct everything like fundraising, getting travel visas, and any vaccinations you might need."

"What do we do while we're in Guatemala?" I asked.

"They call them 'service trips,' but the main thing you do is travel around, meet people, and learn about the communities. Sometimes you end up doing a lot of actual projects, and sometimes you just gain knowledge about the conditions in a third-world country."

I filled out the application, and our group meetings started soon after. We got to know each other, and we all looked forward to our weekly meetings as the trip approached. School let out for the holidays, and I went home for Christmas then drove back to Chicago to meet my group at the airport. It was the middle of a frigid winter, and we all wore thick coats, hats, gloves, and a layer of cold-weather clothes.

With pride, I presented my brand new passport at the airport, which certified me for the international flight. After several flights and layovers, plus an hour-long ride in a van, we finally arrived at San Lucas Toliman, a small town in the mountains. Guatemala is close to the equator and within minutes, we knew that none of our winter clothes would be needed.

Our guide was a man named Juan, and he accompanied us everywhere. Juan was in his late twenties, and he spoke excellent English.

"We are so grateful that Americans come to our city," he told us.

We followed him to the upper floor of a two-story building that had individual rooms with two beds each. He explained how to use the toilet, which was quite different from home.

"Do not put any paper in the toilet," Juan said. "There's not enough water or pressure to flush everything, so put everything in the trash can next to it. Welcome to Guatemala."

We spent most of our time traveling to different communities to learn about life in a third-world country from the people who lived there. On a tour of a coffee plantation, we learned that the annual income for one of their workers was less than one hundred dollars. Yet, everyone seemed very happy, and they appreciated the opportunity to meet some Americans.

The trip to Guatemala was my first taste of international travel, and it was an excellent introduction to foreign adventure. The older, experienced staff members gave us lots of support, and they challenged us to expand our experiences in Guatemala to other countries.

The research step not only helped me figure out how I could travel more, it also taught me how to push toward the work and other experiences that excited me.

Get some experience!

You can always walk away from opportunities if you don't have any experience, but if you do, you'll miss the chance to grow. Great challenge leads to great rewards. The most ineffective way to gain experience is to sit around and wish for it. The easy first step is to get online and start learning.

One of the best ways to get some experience is to become a volunteer, and not just for humanitarian causes like serving the homeless at a soup kitchen. When you put yourself in the position to serve in any role, it can lead to opportunities that may become long-term, paid positions.

And don't underestimate your personal network. Everyone, even the most shy, soft-spoken introvert, has people in their life. And these people know people who know people, and so on. When you talk about what you want to do, you put an intention out to the world, and it can yield incredible results—which is something I still have to remind myself. More often than not, people want to help other people and will be happy to connect you with opportunities when they can.

Actions breed rewards. Research, networking, volunteering, and simply telling other people what you want will bring rewards. It may take some time to see the results, but simple, consistent action builds your confidence and creates momentum. The more you tell others and write about what you want, the more confident you will become. Stick with it long enough, and you'll be surprised who might be attracted to your journey and wants to help with the next steps.

> The more you tell others and write about what you want, the more confident you will become.

The summer circus

When I got back from teaching in Japan, I saw an advertisement from the St. Louis Science Center for a circus camp for kids and trapeze classes for adults. I was working as a DJ on the weekends, and since my days were free, I decided to find out about the camp. I hoped to become involved somehow.

The Science Center is a St. Louis treasure. The massive facility resembles a space station and has three floors of interactive exhibitions on biology, chemistry, and physics. A sheltered walkway extends over the highway, and you can watch the cars whiz by below through sections of glass on the floor. You can even use radar guns to measure their speed.

Behind the main building lies the Exploradome, a gargantuan bubble about the size of a football field that features special exhibits. That summer, the dome served as a circus big top. I asked for the person in charge, and a woman named Julie met me in the lobby outside the entrance. Wearing casual clothes, she looked like an average soccer mom instead of a grand figure who ran a circus exhibition.

"What all is going on here?" I asked.

She proudly explained, "This is Circus Camp! Kids come for a week at a time and work on circus skills."

"What kind of skills" I asked. "Is it just juggling?"

"No, it's everything!" she said. "Juggling, Spinning plates, diabolo, flower sticks, globe-walking, stilt-walking, and a bunch of other things." It sounded like the coolest camp ever, and my heart jumped.

"Do you have a child that's interested?" she asked.

"No, not even close," I chuckled. "I want to see if I can get a job with you."

"I am set with people right now," she answered. "Maybe next year."

That rejection barely registered. "Can I volunteer?" I asked.

Julie saw my enthusiasm and smiled. "What skills do you have?" she asked.

"I can juggle, and I taught myself how to ride a unicycle."

"Come on in, let's see if we can find something for you to do."

We walked through the main doors, and one big playground stretched before us. Kids were moving everywhere, and they worked on different skills just like Julie said. I looked up and saw an expansive set of poles, ladders, ropes, platforms, and a safety net.

"What is that?" I asked.

"A trapeze," Julie said. "We have adult classes at night."

I was awestruck. Kids swung from a platform about thirty feet above the ground, launched themselves into a flip, and fell safely onto the wide net strung high above our head.

"I think I'm in love," I said.

Julie laughed and said, "Come back tomorrow morning. Ride your unicycle around the main lobby. You can tell people about circus camp."

"I would love to!"

"Once we start," she said, "you can come back to the dome and work with the kids. We appreciate your volunteer time, so however long you want to stay is fine."

Even though I wasn't paid, I loved the chance to be with the kids and learn new skills together. That summer, I learned how to spin plates on a stick and balance myself on a giant globe, among many other things. The greatest moment of the summer happened after I'd volunteered for a few weeks.

"Joe," Julie said. "You have spent so much time with us this summer. I wish we could pay you. Would you like to join the trapeze class for free?"

The adult trapeze lessons cost several hundred dollars. She had not even finished the sentence when I blurted out "YES! YES! YES!"

The rest of that summer, I volunteered for a couple hours during the week and went to trapeze class every Monday night. A handful of other men and women had joined the class to try something different, challenging, and fun. I was ready for my first trapeze flight.

I had a fascination with heights, and the tall ladder that looked out over the circus camp appealed to me. A small platform was attached to a thick pole that had enough room for two people: the flyer and the helper. A professional instructor secured my belt with shoulder straps, then he latched on the safety line. I clapped some chalk onto my hands, and he handed me the bar connected to two wires.

I grabbed hold, took one small hop up, and kicked my legs. The trapeze flung me fast and far, and all the sound in that busy dome completely disappeared. I rode the wave of the swinging trapeze and felt completely, totally free. After a few swings, the instructor yelled "Hop!" which was my signal to let go at the apex of the swing. I drifted down like a leaf and nestled into the safety net below, then hustled back up for as many swings as I could get in that night.

By the end of the summer, I had learned several individual tricks on the bar and had even tried partner swinging, where another instructor swung from the other side and caught my hands in mid-flight. Even though I could not make a living on a trapeze, I had found joy in this unique pursuit.

Emboldened by a summer full of circus stunts, I looked for more fun ways to earn a living, but my parents and my new wife had given me subtle hints that I needed to find a conventional office job. By the end of the summer, their hints turned into direct requests. Yet, I was determined to find something I could do that was fun and that I could look forward to. I had talked to people, volunteered, and put my intention out into the world. Something had to turn up.

Make magic

I was flipping through a free, weekly newspaper that had want ads on the back pages, and one ad stuck out. "After School Magic Instructor Wanted," it read. "1-4 hours a week. We teach you the tricks." I didn't know magic, but here was another chance to get in front of people. Immediately, I made the call.

"I don't have any magic experience, but I have some other skills," I told the man on the phone.

"Great," he said. "Come on in for an interview, and we'll go from there."

I went to their office and was interviewed by his assistant. She was about my age, taught some of the classes, and helped him manage the business. She asked about my job history and pulled out a deck of cards.

"This is important," she said. "I'm going to perform a card trick, show you how to do it, then you'll do it for me."

"This is easily the coolest job interview I've had yet," I said.

She smiled and proceeded to show me a classic card trick called "The Four Robbers." I learned it right away, although my performance left a little to be desired.

"No problem," she said. "You've got the basics. We'll be in touch." She said she would call, and I left. A few days later, they hired me.

"First," she said, "you have to observe two classes and then have a follow up interview to see if you're ready.

The first class was at a school on the other side of town. I made the forty-minute drive and found the instructor in his classroom.

"Are you new?" he asked. "I'm Josh."

"I'm Joe," I said. "What do you want me to do?

"Just sit and watch right now. Pretend like you're one of these first graders."

For forty-five minutes, Josh taught these kids the most simple magic tricks. An invisible ball caught in a bag. A jumping rubber band. A disappearing penny. The kids were fascinated. I was hooked.

Josh walked with me out to the car, and asked about my experience.

"Not a lot," I said. "But I can juggle."

"Let me see," he said, and handed me three bean bags.

I showed him some of the tricks I had known since theatre class my freshman year of high school. "And I can ride a unicycle," I said.

"We are going to make beautiful music together." Josh became one of the most important mentors of my career. Not only had he tried what seemed like every skill under the sun in terms of performing, he excelled at every one of them.

The first month I went to an elementary school with Josh, where he performed for two hundred kids in kindergarten through eighth grade. He played that audience like a violin and brought their energy up and down at a steady pace. He mixed his juggling skills with magic tricks, and by the end of the hour, the kids were in a frenzy. They gave him a thunderous standing ovation. That event became my image for my next job.

After the show, I asked, "Can you teach me how to do what you just did?"

"Sure, the tricks aren't hard," he said with a shrug.

"No, the performance part, too. I have always wanted to do what you just did."

"I'll show you everything," Josh said.

Over the next year, Josh and our main boss worked with me to create a show. At the beginning, my main strength was juggling, and we incorporated a few magic tricks into a routine. Gradually, Josh and I became our company's main two performers. We entertained at schools, preschools, libraries, camps, and birthday parties. With every show, my experience grew, and I loved this good path.

For the first two years, the few bills my wife and I had were paid, and I enjoyed the work that allowed us to pay them. Even though I mainly worked on weekend nights, Michiyo was happy that I was enjoying myself and my work. However, she saw it all as temporary.

"How long are you going to do this?" she asked.

"I'd like to do it until I can't pay the bills anymore," I told her.

"How long will that be?" she said.

"Two, maybe three years," I answered. She wasn't totally happy with that answer but went along with it for the moment.

Josh eventually went out on his own, and I became the main performer and lead man. I had loyal clients and produced lots of business with classes and shows, and on the music side of things, I was the most requested DJ in St. Louis.

When I started out, I envisioned making a living by entertaining people in St. Louis. My confidence, consistent action, and a lot of persistence allowed me to overcome my lack of experience, but once I got the experience, the results were directly in line with my long-term vision about the type of work I wanted to do.

The interview test

Too often, we overlook the experience we do have and, instead, focus on what we don't have. We might think we haven't even taken the first step, when in fact we actually took that step long ago. The truth is that your life is made up of many different segments, and those segments are all connected, whether you can see it or not. But once you see the connections, you can recognize the valuable experience you already have and turn it into an asset.

When I decided to teach English in Japan, I knew nothing about that country, but I applied anyway. The only two requirements were that I had to have a college degree and had to be a native English speaker. I qualified on both points. The next step was to send in my application, complete with transcripts and letters of recommendation. I did so and was invited for an interview.

Before the interview, I was concerned because I didn't have any teaching experience, but then I realized that I actually had all the experience I needed, even at the age of twenty-three. I had been in hundreds of strangers' homes and given sales presentations about knives. How much different could teaching in Asia be? And I had studied Chinese in high school and Spanish in college. Granted, Japanese would be different, but I liked the challenge of a new language. I went to the interview confident that I had plenty of experience.

The interview was on my birthday, and I went to the Japanese Consulate in Kansas City. I met with a panel of three people. They interviewed me in a small conference room that had a whiteboard in the front of the room. A man and a woman who appeared to be only a few years older than me sat at the table. An older woman with glasses and gray hair sat between them. The younger two seemed happy and polite, but the older woman didn't crack a smile. If the interviewers were playing a good cop/bad cop game, I spotted the bad cop in a hurry.

"Tell us what you hope to gain by living in Japan," the younger woman said.

"I don't know anything about living in Asia, and I thought this would be a great opportunity to do that," I said.

"Have you taught before?" asked the man.

"Not technically, but I have held several leadership positions in school, and I taught salespeople for several years in my business," I told him.

A few more questions from the younger two made me feel good. Then the older woman chimed in.

"I see here that you traveled to Europe and went to a number of countries in a short time," she began.

I got excited because I thought my international experience was my main asset. "Yes, I learned a lot."

She turned the tables on me. "I'm concerned that you only spent a few days in each country. You are applying for a position that is a year long. How do you know you won't want to leave after a little while?"

At first, a small panic rose up. She was right. The backpacking trip taught me a lot, but it was quite different from this position. Fortunately, I had thought a lot about this before the interview.

"You raise a good point," I said. "That trip was my first experience on another continent. I learned a lot, but, in particular, I realized how much I don't know. So I am looking forward to embracing life in Japan in a way that I couldn't experience in such a short time in Europe. Even if I am miserable, I have no plans to leave before the year is over."

She sat silently, still with no smile. The younger woman spoke up again.

"Let's do role play. Pretend that we're in a classroom in Japan, and you are asked to present a lesson on your favorite holiday back home," she said.

I sat back and took a second to think. I pictured my sales training where we had role-played during those eventful college summers. At first I'd played the salesman, then I switched to being the customer who threw out objections that my partner had to address. I felt ready for this challenge, but I wanted to clarify a few details.

"What supplies do I have for this exercise?" I asked.

"Whatever you want, just pretend the supplies you need are next to you," the younger woman said.

"How much English do you all know?" I asked.

"None," the older woman said firmly.

"And how much Japanese do I know?" I asked.

"How much Japanese do you know now?" the older woman asked in a sour tone.

"None," I said.

"Please begin," she said.

I started slow, and stumbled over a few words, but then built some momentum.

"My favorite holiday is Christmas," I said and wrote the words 'Merry Christmas' on the board. "Everyone say 'Christmas.'"

All three said, "Christmas."

"I love Christmas because it's in winter, when there is lots of snow on the ground." I drew a big hill and some snow flakes. "I love to go sled riding," I told them. "On Christmas morning, everyone gets presents. Santa brings presents." I spoke slow and clear, since these "students" couldn't understand my words. "Everyone say, 'Santa.'"

They all said, "Santa."

"In fact, I brought some presents for all of you." I figured that if there was no limit on my imaginary supplies, I should go all out. I went through the motions of picking up presents and placed them in front of each interviewer. I had no idea where this routine would go, then inspiration hit. "Open them up," I said with hand motions. "Everybody gets, um, an American flag!"

The two younger people smiled and waved their invisible American flag like excited little children. The older woman sat silently and seemed disappointed that I had done a good job. I waited for the next directive and rejoiced inside. I had enjoyed that bit of make-believe and considered my performance admirable, given the on-the-spot directions.

"Thank you Mr. Fingerhut," the man said. "You may go now. You'll receive a letter about your status in the next month."

"Thank you. Have a nice day," I told them, and headed toward the door.

"Oh, and Joe," the younger woman said with a sweet smile. I knew she had enjoyed the fake lesson on Christmas. "Happy Birthday."

"Thanks," I said, and walked out the door.

When I got to my friend's apartment where I was staying that night, he wanted to hear about everything.

"How'd it go?" he asked.

"Book the ticket!" I yelled, and gave him a high five.

A few months after that, I boarded a plane to fly to my new home in Kumamoto City, Japan.

My grand Japanese adventure lasted three years. I knew I could go after anything I wanted, regardless of my experience. From one perspective, I started with very little experience. But from another, I had a very solid foundation of experiences and skills that made everything possible and served me well. After that, I never let a lack of experience prevent me from trying something new.

EXCUSE BUSTER:

No experience? No problem—do it anyway!

Ask:

1. How is your lack of experience holding you back from pursuing something you'd like to do?
2. How often do you share your big goal or dream with people in your life?
3. Where can you volunteer that allows you to do that exact thing you want to do, even if you don't get paid for it?
4. Do you find reasons to say "no" to things instead of "yes?" What are those reasons?

Act:

1. Write down one of your aspirations or goals. Examples: Is there a team you want to make? A school club you want to join (theatre/band/newspaper)? A certain college you want to attend? A part-time job you want?
2. List one resource, person, or organization that could help you achieve that goal. Examples: Head/Assistant Coach, Advisor, Admissions office, Application Manager.
3. This week, contact that person either by phone, email, snail mail, social media, or all of these methods. Tell them what you want to do, and ask what you can do to help THEM.

Excuse 7

I Don't Know Anyone Else Who Has Done This

Psychology 101 was one of my favorite college classes. Several hundred students sat in stadium-style seats in an auditorium with just one professor who lectured to a sea of students. It was really easy to sneak in late.

It was a course about how people think, and it featured enough interesting lessons that I considered making Psychology my major. I ultimately chose Math as my major, but two specific lessons that I learned in Psych class have stuck with me to this day.

The first is that human beings repeat relationships.

Our professor told us that if a girl suffered physical abuse by her father, she had a high probability of choosing abusive relationships later on. I thought about that kind of repeated pattern in my own life, only it wasn't about abuse. My mom always got along so well with kids, and that example influenced my own preferences in relationships. I was always drawn to women with a teaching background, and I eventually married a preschool teacher.

The second principle is that we gravitate toward people who have similar backgrounds. Our professor talked about how children of divorced parents tend to gravitate toward others whose parents are also divorced. My group of friends at the time illustrated that point in opposite terms: Most of our parents were still married after many years. I had never noticed this dynamic until it was pointed out in class. Because I had living proof, I quickly saw that these principles also surfaced when getting to know someone. Their past often predicts their future.

But when you are pursuing something new and exciting, those very principles can work against you. Let's say you're inspired by a career or an unconventional, short-term experience. If you don't know anyone else who has done it, it could become an excuse for not doing it yourself.

I came from a family of teachers, and it would have made perfect sense for me to become a teacher, too. Dad never cared that I choose any specific career, but he would have fully supported a teaching career because it offered dependable hours and job security. When he tried to shoot down my Europe aspirations, it was because he wanted me to pursue something more conventional. Getting out of America to see the world seemed way out of my league. None of my immediate family members and only two of my cousins had ever been out of the country, and we had a big family.

Just because your circle doesn't know anything about what you want to do, that doesn't mean that you can't do it. There are over six billion people on earth, and the chances are high that someone, somewhere has already done what you want to do. Find a way to connect with them, or at the very least, learn more about them, and they can help show you how to do it yourself. Most people love to talk about what they've done and what they've learned, so ask them! If they don't know about that particular subject, they may know someone else who can help you. It's your job to seek out this expertise and to connect with people who can help.

Cousin Krista comes through

When I decided go to Europe, I felt like I was alone on an island; not one member of my immediate family had ever done anything like backpacking around another continent. I was discouraged because I wasn't connected with anyone who'd had such an experience.

My mom mentiond that my cousin, Krista, had traveled and studied abroad a bit. Krista attended family functions, celebrations, and picnics, but we had never talked about travel before. So I called her and told her about what I wanted to do.

"That sounds like an amazing adventure!" Krista said. "One of the best things you can do at your age to learn more about the world is to travel."

"I'm excited," I said, "but also nervous. How did you know where to go and what to do?"

"I spent a semester in Italy. Europe is so easy to get around, and I did plenty of traveling."

"I've read about the trains."

"I love the trains! I wish we had a system like the Eurail in America. Those trains go everywhere."

"One of the best things you can do at your age to learn more about the world is to travel."

"How did you know where to stay?" I asked.

"There's a guidebook series called *Let's Go!* They have different versions for different countries and continents."

"So the guidebook was really useful?" I asked.

"I couldn't have gotten along without it. It tells you what to see, where to eat, and where to sleep, and where to find cheap options for everything."

I scribbled down the details and felt immediate excitement. "Did you spend a lot of money, or were things pretty cheap?"

"Things were usually less expensive than in America, but not crazy cheap. When you talk to people, you'll find ways to save money, plus the guidebooks help," she said.

"Do they have these books at the library?" I asked.

Her response was perfect. "I think I still have mine," she said. "It's a couple of years old, but the information is still good. You can have it."

Unbelievable—somebody related to me knew about this stuff!

"And, Joe," Krista added, "no matter what, you have to do this. None of our parents have ever done something like this. I bet your mom and dad are freaking out."

"You are completely right," I confirmed.

"I can tell you from experience, it will all be fine. Go for it!"

We eventually crossed paths, and Krista gave me the book. Just like she said, this thick and heavy resource had tons of useful information about the best places to go, how to get there, and how to do everything on the cheap.

I didn't expect that the guidebook would create a problem the night before my flight to Paris, but my backpack was crammed, and it added extra weight and took up a lot of space. I thought about all the notes I'd taken and the information stored in my head. *Let's make this a real adventure,* I thought, and tossed it aside.

Because I left that book at home, every day became an exciting reason to connect with local people who knew places better than any book ever would. I struck up numerous conversations with fellow backpackers who had their own guidebooks, and I got to know even more people because I asked for their recommendations.

Now, whenever I have the opportunity to get to know someone, I always ask them about their jobs, travel, hobbies, and family, which has led to fascinating experiences that I wouldn't have had otherwise.

On March 11, 2011, an earthquake off the coast of Japan produced a thirty-foot tsunami. The wave destroyed entire cities along the coast and damaged towns many miles inland. An inconceivable volume of water rushed in, around, and through every man-made object in sight. The news footage from that terrifying day took viewers' breath away.

Unbelievably, within a few hours, the water was gone. The ocean receded back to its normal level, like nothing had happened. In its wake, a wasteland of toppled buildings, shattered houses, and discolored vehicles remained, along with piles of unrecognizable clutter. The Japanese who lived in those areas had to rebuild their lives and start from scratch.

When we're struck by a new idea, excitement can hit us with the force of a tsunami, and this new inspiration can take over our minds and dominate our thoughts. These ideas create more ideas, and we are inspired to make them happen.

Like a tsunami, however, that inspiration can be short-lived. When the initial rush wears off, we have to figure out where to start and what to do next, just like the Japanese had to do. A powerful idea must be built from the ground up.

In Japan, they called in the experts. The local residents picked through rubble, swept up waste, and cleared roads, but they needed professional crews to clear out the debris and build new structures. Because so much had been destroyed by the disaster, these crews had to be called in from outside the immediate area.

Connect with an expert

When an idea hits you like a tsunami, it's a good idea to connect with experts. It's too overwhelming to try to find solutions on your own. When you find people who have already gone through the building-up process, you can apply their knowledge and experience to your own situation. The good news is that you don't have to endure a tsunami to find that path. To be a successful entertainer, I had to find the experts. I had to connect with other entertainers or with people who knew them.

> When you find people who have already gone through the building-up process, you can apply their knowledge and experience to your own situation.

Jubilee is the national magic conference held in St. Louis, where performers from all over the country gather to network, learn new material, and absorb information from the experts. I threw all care aside and introduced myself to everyone I could. One guy wasn't actually a professional entertainer, although he had done some performing in his younger years. He evaluated my situation as a newly married guy who had fun making people laugh. His advice was direct and succinct.

"Get a job, pay your bills, and have fun with magic as a hobby," he said.

We talked for a bit, and he bragged about how much money he'd made as an architect after he stopped doing magic as a kid. Then he pointed to a man across the room. He was bald, of medium height, and looked classy, but not fancy, in his black shirt and black pants.

"You could be like him," my new friend said with a tone of awe. "He makes twenty thousand dollars an hour giving speeches to corporations."

"Who is he, and what does he do?" I asked, excited to be in the same room with someone of that caliber. I figured he was from California or New York.

"His name is Shep Hyken, and he lives right here in St. Louis. He's a motivational speaker."

I was thrilled to know that someone in St. Louis had a successful career doing the very thing I had wanted to do since college. Too intimidated to approach him at the conference, I looked up his information and called him a few days later. Shep agreed to sit down with me for thirty minutes. His office was very understated, a simple suite in a large office building.

"Come on in!" he said in a friendly tone. "How can I help you?"

"I want to be a speaker," I told him. "You're the most successful speaker I know." I didn't tell him he was actually one of the only speakers I knew.

"What will you speak about?" he asked.

"I backpacked through Europe after college, lived in Japan for three years, and now I do magic, juggling, and DJ on the weekends. I want to tell kids to follow their dreams," I said.

"When you say kids, what do you mean?" he asked.

"College kids, maybe, but probably high school kids."

"So teens are your target?"

"I guess. I don't know for sure," I said.

Shep took it from there. He told me how he got started and that he targeted corporations where he could speak about customer service. As he got more successful, he raised his fee, took fewer engagements, and had more time to spend with his family.

"It's a long process, and you spend a lot of time away from home," he cautioned.

He gave me some tips on how to generate business. Call schools. Find out who hires their speakers and ask them to give me a shot. Network with other speakers.

I had one final question. "Are you happy with your lifestyle?" I asked.

"I've been doing this twenty-five years," Shep said. "I play hockey twice a week and get plenty of family time. I'm about to finish my third book. I love speaking, and my clients support me. I love my lifestyle."

"Is there anything I can do for you?" I asked in parting.

"Show me forward progress."

With that, I thanked him, and he wished me luck.

Act as if!

When I was in college, I saw the movie *Boiler Room,* a story about stock traders who tricked eager investors into investing in fake companies. Granted, the characters were seedy, but I learned several valuable lessons from the film.

One of them was to "act as if."

In one scene, Ben Affleck advised a soft-spoken, young associate how to improve his phone conversations. "ACT AS IF!" he shouts in anger. "You need to *act as if* you are the vice president of this firm!"

It was a lesson in gaining confidence, and I started to notice that people respond to people who have confidence. If we project confidence, people assume competence. If we stick with it long enough, our confidence will match our competence, and at that point, the magic starts to happen.

After about a year of being a DJ, I had made some progress. Several clients requested me, and I became more comfortable with handling all the tasks at a big party. My performance reflected my level of competence, and yet my confidence lagged behind.

Every quarter, our company offered seminars to teach us how we could improve. During those meetings, they would announce the Top Ten DJs, based on the number of times clients had requested them. I knew I was just as skilled, if not better than, most of the other DJs; however, the numbers didn't back me up yet.

After one of the seminars, I talked to Ted Burke, one of the most requested DJs in St. Louis. Ted had been in the business for nearly two decades and had learned to straddle that fine line between making people laugh and making them cringe, and he often made himself the butt of his own jokes. He had a physical problem that caused him to sweat. A lot. A ton. So he called himself "Sweaty Teddy," and that nickname fit him like a glove. He had turned this shortcoming into a strength.

"When do you know you're good?" I asked him.

"When people want you to be their DJ," he said.

"I get requested a little bit, and my parties usually turn out great."

"So what's the problem?" he asked.

"I finish these receptions, and I know I did a good job. The bride, groom, and their families all say what a great time they had. They go out of their way to tell me that!"

"Sounds like things are working for you," he said.

"But then I drive home and wonder if I did a good job. I think about what I could have done better and try to figure out how I can get more people to request me."

Ted thought about what I said for a second. He shifted his body so that he faced me.

"Look at me," Ted commanded. "There is a plaque on that wall that names every number one DJ in this company's history. There is no reason you shouldn't be on that wall."

"Okay," I said and nodded with a little uncertainty. "I should be on that wall."

"Stop doubting yourself. This is not rocket science. We show up, play music, have fun with people, give them a great time, then pack up and go home. You are excellent at this."

"I feel pretty good about what I do," I said.

"Then ACT like it! People have more respect for you if you're sure of yourself. Stop wondering. You're great. Decide to see yourself as a great DJ. Don't be arrogant, just confident."

After that, I adopted an air of confidence. When they announced the Top Ten at our next meeting, my name wasn't at the top spot, but I had made the list for the first time. I came in at number ten.

"Congratulations, Mr. Top Ten!" Teddy said with a slap on the back.

"Thanks," I said. "I'm on the list but not number one."

"Doesn't matter. Keep doing what you're doing, and you'll get there."

I continued to put myself out there, and people noticed. The calls rolled in each quarter, and I moved up the list. Just one year after Ted gave me that pep talk, I held the #1 trophy. I had acted like the best DJ for so long that my attitude finally matched my skills. Confidence had caught up to competence .

EXCUSE BUSTER:

Don't know anyone? Get out there and meet people, connect, and network!

Ask:

1. Are you drowning in ideas of things you should do but feel overwhelmed and can't pick one to start?
2. What do you WANT to do?
3. Name a family member or friend who has done it.
4. If you don't have any family members or friends who have done it, what are some other ways you could connect with people who have that experience?
5. Name some areas where you could ACT more confident?
6. How does your uncertainty make you appear less competent?

Act:

1. Write down the name of one person (they can be a celebrity, but they must be living), who does the kind of work you'd like to do.
2. Do everything you can to find their contact information: phone, address, email, or social media information. Reach out to them through one of these methods.
3. Keep your communication short. Tell them what you want to know, and be sincere. Example: "I'm a fan. I would love to do what you do. How did you get started?"
4. Wait a week. If you don't get a response, identify another person and repeat this process.

Excuse 8

I Can't Do This. It's Too Hard!

Whatever the mind of man can conceive and believe, it can achieve.
Napolean Hill

In Japan, I normally taught English at the junior high schools, but sometimes I was scheduled for a day at a local elementary school. On one of those days, I walked outside for recess and saw the strangest phenomenon.

About twenty-five six-year-olds were RIDING UNICYCLES! And they were good. More than good. It looked like they'd been doing it since they could walk. Or even before! These happy, smiling kids rolled along and reveled in the shocked look on their American teacher's face.

"Hello Joe sensei!" they screamed with glee. "Konnichiwa!"

How can I?

My first reaction was that you could never do this in America because of the lawsuits. I could picture parents going crazy over such a dangerous activity and calling their lawyers when their precious little Johnny conked his head or scratched his arm.

My second thought was more personal. *How can I do that?*

I had never, not once in life, thought about riding a unicycle. But these kids rode as easily as they breathed. It didn't look easy, and I had scant optimism that I could do it.

At first I tried to use the first graders' unicycles, but they were too small. I kept my eye out for bigger ones at the other schools but found nothing. My tiny network of friends and co-workers didn't know where to buy or even borrow a unicycle.

I stumbled onto a bike shop just outside downtown Kumamoto and saw a shiny, yellow unicycle in the window. It gleamed in the sunlight. Adult-sized, it came up to my shoulders, and shouted, "BUY ME!"

I went inside and wondered whether I would, could, or even should buy it. The shopkeeper, very excited to see an American in his store, came right over.

"You buy unicycle?" he asked in simple English.

"Oh, no thank you," I said. "Too hard."

"No, no!" he protested. "You get this. Just need practice."

I took another look. The little kids rode tiny unicycles that were shorter than my legs. This one came up to my ears! I couldn't escape the feeling that I was supposed to do this.

"How much?" I asked.

"Two thousand, five hundred," he said, and began to take it off the rack.

"Wait a minute! I don't have that much!"

He looked at me. On the other side of the unicycle, there was a sign written in Japanese that had a red border around it. It said 2,500, and I repeated the number out loud.

"Two thousand, five hundred," he said. "Yen."

I was still new to Japan and struggled with many things, including the conversion of money. Then it hit me. "Two thousand five hundred yen is only about twenty bucks American!" I shouted.

The shopkeeper didn't understand, but he got the point. He took it down, went to the cash register, and sold a unicycle that was on clearance.

I took it the out on my first day of spring break. Behind my apartment building, there was a tall, steel fence that bordered an elementary school, and it had plenty of places where I could hold on.

I planted my left foot on the pedal closest to the ground, and grasped the fence railing with one hand. My other hand held the seat in place, right at my midsection. I took a deep breath and hoisted myself up on the seat, about four or five feet off the ground. *Now all I have to do is move forward,* I said to myself.

I gripped the fence railing and my arms bore the entire weight of my body. My feet clung to the pedals and my legs hugged the long, thin metal tube on which the seat rested. I didn't know that riding a unicycle meant that all parts of my body had to act in unison. It strained my upper body, my lower body, and my core to move only a few inches. As uncomfortable as it was, I was determined to keep trying. I inched along and worked my way along the railing until it ended at a driveway. I turned around and made my way back to the starting point, continuing for about an hour. I hadn't made much progress, but I was happy with my effort and felt good about the prospects for the rest of the week.

The next day, I began the same way. Feet on pedals, hands on railing, everything in balance, and away I went. I made minuscule improvement, but my pride in this accomplishment was short-lived. After about twenty minutes, I felt a twinge in my back. I walked home slowly, aware that something bad had just happened.

Sure enough, when I woke up the next morning, I could barely move. Any slight motion was like plunging a knife into my back. For two days I'd used muscles I didn't even know I had, and the resulting strain rendered me motionless. I called my supervisor. Even though school was out for spring break, we were supposed to report to the school board office every day.

"I hurt my back," I said.

"Is everything okay?" he asked.

"Yes," I said, but left out the part about the unicycle. "I just can't move."

He was silent for a few seconds, then said, "We will come and take you to the hospital."

"Okay, that sounds good," I said and meant it. I would do anything for relief.

We made the short ride, and my supervisor took care of the administrative details. I was so thankful to have him there, since I could not communicate with the doctors.

Within half an hour, I was sprawled out on a bed getting a thorough and deep back massage. The pain still throbbed and did not go away, but it subsided enough to allow me to move around a little bit. After I confessed about how I was injured, the doctor and my supervisor suggested I lay off unicycle practice for a while, and I did.

A month later, I went back to the railing. I decided I would only practice for fifteen minutes, which I did a couple times one week, followed by a few weeks off. Over time, I made gradual improvement and told a friend about it.

"How's the unicycle going? You've been doing it forever," he said.

"It's slow going, but I'm getting it," I said.

"Are you almost there?"

"At first I could ride smoothly while holding on to the railing with one hand. Now I can let go for a few feet," I said. "I only practice for fifteen minutes at a time."

My progress was incremental, and I tried not to focus on the short-term grind. I pictured myself making an effortless ride across the parking lot.

One sunny afternoon, long after that first spring break, I found two posts that were about ten feet apart, but didn't have a railing to connect them. I mounted the unicycle, took a deep breath, let go, and fell right off. I got up again, started to pedal forward, and fell again after a few feet. I got on one more time, and let go. My eyes were laser focused on the post ten feet away, and my legs pedaled me there. I grabbed the post in victory, and adrenaline rushed through every cell of my body. I didn't want to get too excited and forced myself to keep practicing. I covered the same ground a few more times, then called it a day. I was happy, but not satisfied.

Every time I went back to practice, I set a new benchmark: twenty feet, then thirty. Finally, a few days later, I told myself to not think about where to stop. I put one foot on the bottom pedal, raised my body up onto the seat, breathed in, let go, and looked straight ahead. I pedaled and pedaled all the way across the parking lot, into the street, and down the block!

I jumped off, stunned, not even sure what just happened. My vision had come true: I had ridden a unicycle down the street! I was a unicycle rider. A unicyclist. Mission accomplished!

Of course, I didn't stop there. That small bit of confidence made me even more motivated to improve. It took two years to learn to ride like a six-year old. At the beginning, I thought I could never do this. Now I pedaled around, just like I envisioned. Success felt good.

Achieving that goal taught me what success requires: steady, consistent action.

I've enjoyed success in many different areas, but what has built my confidence the most was learning to ride that unicycle. Achieving that goal taught me what success requires: steady, consistent action.

Doubts

I am not good enough.
I am not rich enough.
I am not handsome enough.
My nose is too big.
My ears stick out too much.
My eyes don't look right.
I am too small.
I am not smart enough.

Have you ever said things like that to yourself? That's your *resistant voice*. Almost everyone doubts themselves, but successful people do great things despite what their resistance voice tells them.

That voice in my head frequently told me that when everyone else thought I would fail, they were probably right. I soon learned that everyone has their own resistance voice, but I decided that I could work through the self-doubt that accompanies—and can crush—my ambitions. Dealing with that doubt allowed me to toss it aside and charge forward.

> Almost everyone doubts themselves, but successful people do great things despite what their resistance voice tells them.

Having doubts is not the exception, it's the rule.

As a kid, Dad would watch professional basketball games with me, and he pointed out the greatness of Larry Bird, explaining the nuances of the game. Later on, Michael Jordan became my favorite player, and after that, I was hooked. As Michael's career came to a close, I followed the new wave of talent.

One post-Jordan player was Vince Carter, an extraordinary athlete from the University of North Carolina. Not only did he come from UNC like Michael, he also had a bald head and was an incredible jumper. His acrobatic dunks earned him the nickname "Half-Man, Half-Amazing."

Vince's unofficial debut was at the 2000 NBA All-Star Weekend, about halfway through the season. The most anticipated event was the Dunk Contest, and Vince was the star. He executed four dunks that had never been done before, and the arena exploded! Vince made these feats look effortless. He exhibited such grace that I thought he had the ultimate confidence and had done such things countless times.

Then I read an article about that event a few years later. Vince said he had never practiced any of those dunks. He had dunked in games before and for fun, but that contest featured unique versions that were not easy to do. He said he'd had serious doubts about himself before the contest. I was shocked. After that, when he appeared in the newspapers, in books, and on screens large and small, he said, "I was just Vince. I was just the kid from Daytona who could jump high."

A few years ago, my mom retired and ended a long and successful teaching career. For more than three decades, she chugged through school year after school year as the best educator she knew how to be. And her students loved her.

"You were always good at it, right?" I asked.

"Not at all, Joe."

"What do you mean?"

"I always thought I wasn't good enough," she said. "I always had this fear that someday, somebody would come in my classroom and call my bluff. They would laugh at my credentials and say, 'You aren't qualified to teach these kids,' and I would be exposed."

That revelation hit home. It was one thing for Vince Carter to tell a reporter about his self-doubt. But if my mom, who was one of the most solid influences in my life, doubted her credibility, then maybe it was normal to doubt myself, too.

If you have doubts, it isn't a sign that you shouldn't do something; it's normal to feel doubt. But you can't let your doubts stop you. I finally had to reach a point where I was comfortable with doubt, as long as what I was doing was worthwhile. I did it anyway.

Why not me?

I was a math major and a logical thinker, and I reasoned that if everyone feels doubt to some degree, then the question to ask isn't "Why me?" but "Why NOT me?" That attitude helped me land a job in Japan, master the unicycle, and explore a number of other foreign countries.

It also contributed to my early speaking success. I wasn't totally confident about the quality of my web site or my speaking video, two critical elements that I'd been told were essential to get speaking engagements. I was filled with doubt, so I hesitated to reach out to prospective clients. Doubts or not, I figured I would find out if I was qualified or not when I put myself out there. I also thought that plenty of other speakers probably had doubts about their own products, so why not go for it? And then I got a few bookings based on the materials I already had—enough to let me know that what I had was good enough to get started—and I built my speaking career from that foundation.

Make a victory list

The good news is that you can decide how long your spells of doubt last. And there's a simple action you can take to cut them short: make a list of your accomplishments.

The list could be short and only feature your major feats, such as graduating high school or college, getting picked for a school play or a sports team, or flying on a plane for the first time. If you want to re-affirm your self-worth, the list could be more extensive and include every victory you can think of, from learning to ride a bike to asking someone to go to prom.

We tend to have short memories, and making a list will remind you of your accomplishments that you take for granted. Taking stock of your victories confirms your own credibility and restores your confidence, which is key to moving forward to the next thing.

When I was in college, a friend gave me a book by Patrick Combs called *Major in Success.*

"You've got to read this," my friend told me. It was a paperback book with a guy on the cover who was frozen in mid-air, holding a book in his hand.

"Major in Success," I read the title out aloud. "What's it about?"

"It talks about how to make the most of your college years, and how to get a good job afterward."

"All right, I'll take a look," I said.

The book explained how the author tried different things in college and landed some amazing opportunities afterward, and how he ultimately became a professional speaker. I read it pretty quickly and, from time to time, came back to it again for motivation.

A few months later, Patrick Combs came to speak at our school, and I made sure to get there early. Just like his book had, Patrick talked about different strategies that were available to students, like how to study abroad, secure internships, and use the guidance counselors.

But when Patrick emphasized our opportunities in life, he sounded different from anyone I had ever heard before. The way he framed the language and presented his perspective mesmerized me. I was hooked. I knew that what Patrick had just done—motivated me and the other students to action—was at the top of my list for my own career. Afterward, I introduced myself, asked him to sign my copy of his book, and promised to keep in touch. He told me that only about three percent of people that he talked to followed through and actually contacted him after a speaking engagement.

Then I started hearing voices. My strong resistance voice told me I was too young, too inexperienced, and way too uninteresting to even think about becoming a motivational speaker.

And I listened to it.

Over the next few years, I did everything possible to make life interesting. For more than a decade, all I wanted to do was be like Patrick, to get in front of people, and to tell them that their life could be

"I don't really know what I would talk about," I told my sister Katie. "I don't have that much experience," I said.

"Maybe you should just work for ten years, and then you'll have something to say," she answered.

I shuddered at the thought.

Instead, I made a list of my personal victories and significant accomplishments, with separate sections for grade school, high school, college, and post-college. The question I asked myself was: *What skills or accomplishments took a lot of effort for me to achieve that I've now forgotten about or take for granted?*

My list was extensive, and here is a handful of examples:

Grade School:
Learned to read, write, and ride a bike
Played baseball, soccer, basketball, volleyball, track and field
Scored six goals in one soccer game, always led the team in scoring
Graduated from grade school
Applied to and got accepted into the best high school I knew

High School:
Made the soccer team in the first tryout
Learned how to juggle three balls, best juggler in class
Made first cuts in basketball tryouts (major victory even though I didn't make the team)
Learned how to pole vault, cleared ten feet
Tried out for six school teams, got cut from all of them
Got parts in two of the three plays I tried out for
Learned how to call and talk to a girl, ask her out
Learned how to date someone
Attended four proms in senior year
Graduated in the top fifteen percent of my class in a tough academic environment
Got accepted to eight of ten colleges I applied for
Chose to live in Chicago for college

College:
Learned how to live away from home
Three years as a Resident Assistant
Saw Michael Jordan play in person four times
Learned how to succeed in sales
Did stand-up comedy, school mascot
Helped my brother become the mascot at his school
Did community service, led retreats
Took service trip to Guatemala, hiked up a volcano
Graduated College

After College:
Backpacked through Europe
Started and ended my own business, worked out of debt
Lived in Japan for three years, saved money, learned the language
Travelled all over, got my brother to join me
Taught myself how to ride a unicycle
Met, dated, and proposed to Michiyo
Planned and enjoyed two weddings (Japan and USA), honeymooned
    across South America
Started a career as a DJ, magician, juggler, won awards
Traveled with Michiyo, bought and rehabbed a house
Became a dad, twice!

Making this list silenced that resistance voice and helped me think about what I wanted to do with my life and the audience I wanted to reach. Patrick Combs' example drove my vision of reaching young people, high school and college students, in particular.

My list also helped me see that I had a ton of experience from which I could speak, share, and help, and it clarified how I could best serve other people. Using the list, I determined which skill or accomplishment could inspire and encourage other people, and I came up with some topics I could speak about.

I was on my way.

EXCUSE BUSTER:

You can do it! Take a positive look at yourself, and use your track record to give yourself credit for who you are and what you've already done!

Ask:

1. Are you trying to do too many things at once?
2. What does your resistance voice tell you?
3. Do you doubt yourself? Why?

Act:

1. Make a list of your personal victories. Start by writing down five of your achievements in the last five years, then expand your list to include more of your accomplishments. Give yourself credit for what you've done!
2. Use a pen and paper to make two lists. On the first list, write down the most common things you hear your resistance voice say (Example: I'm not tall enough, good looking enough, cool enough, etc.). On the second list, write down the opposite statements.
3. Cross out every line in the first list. Rip it up and throw it away.
4. For one week, read your second list out loud in front of a mirror, twice a day—once when you get up and once before bed.
5. For the entire week, you may not say ANYTHING to criticize yourself (Example: "I'm an idiot," "I am a slob," "I am not good looking"). Find positive alternatives to speak out loud, or don't say anything at all.
6. At the end of the week, write down how you feel about yourself. Has there been any change?

Excuse 9

If I Do This, I'll Miss Out On Something Else

Change is hard. But why?

I believe that it's not the effort to make a change that holds you back, it's the uncertainty of what life will be like once that change is made. We cannot know the future. Even if we think we've considered all the possibilities of what a change might mean, life has a peculiar way of throwing curves that were never on our radar.

> Even if we think we've considered all the possibilities of what a change might mean, life has a peculiar way of throwing curves that were never on our radar.

An age-old axiom holds a lot of truth: "Better the devil you know than the devil you don't know." In other words, things might not be so great right now, but they could turn out far worse if you changed anything, so better stay on the present course and deal with the old, familiar problems.

That kind of thinking will crush you.

The truth is that, whether you like it or not, things will change anyway. It could be slow and subtle, or things might explode all at once. Either way, there's a 100 percent probability that things will change. Once we accept that life is going to happen regardless of our whereabouts, we can face the fear of change with more confidence.

Goodbye to Grandma

Before I went to Europe, Dad made a list of prudent concerns. Somewhere on that list was the possibility that one of my grandparents might die while I was in a foreign country. At the time, three of my four grandparents were still alive, and they were all over age eighty. None of them were in poor health.

"What if something happens to Grandma Millie while you are over there?" Dad asked. "You're not gonna fly back for it, are you? You would miss everything!"

I let that question marinate for a long time and talked to my older cousin, David, about the concern.

"Go anyway," he said. "If she dies, she dies."

"That sounds so cold," I said.

"Well, that's life. That's what happens."

"So what do I do?"

"Give her as much time and attention as you can while you are here. What will you really miss if you're not here when she passes?"

"Well, the funeral," I said.

"Yes, you will miss the funeral, but she'll gone by then. Make the most of your time with her now, then go enjoy your trip, no matter what."

I drove to Grandma Millie's house, a two-story, two-unit brick building. She and Grandpa Joe had raised five kids on the first floor of this structure. They had never moved or gotten a bigger place. I had spent a lot of time in this house as a kid and still could not figure out how they brought up four boys and a girl in such a constricted space.

Grandma Millie was still technically mobile, but for the most part, she stayed in her recliner in the front room. Her mind was as sharp as ever.

"Grandma, I am taking this crazy trip soon," I told her.

"Crazy? Tell me all about it," she said.

"After graduation, I am going to fly to Europe and backpack around for about three months."

"Have you looked into all the details?" she asked.

"Yes. I am pretty sure I can pay for it, and it seems like people have done it before and had good experiences."

158

"What do your parents think?" she said.

"They're not that excited about it."

Grandma smiled. "Then they are feeling exactly how they should."

"What do you think?" I asked.

"Why do you ask?"

"Well, three months is a long time. I don't want to be gone for too long. I won't see you for a while."

"You lived in Kansas City last year. You went to college in Chicago before that. You barely see me anyway, and that's fine. You've got a lot going on," she said.

"Yes, but this time I'll be far away for so long, and you never know what's going to happen."

We didn't say much for a few seconds.

"That sounds amazing. You're gonna love it," she said, assuring me. "You go have a great time." She patted my hand, smiled, and changed the subject.

Soon after, Dad and I sat at our kitchen table and discussed more details about Europe.

"So what about grandparents?" Dad asked.

"I talked to Grandma Millie," I said. "She's fine with me going."

"Of course that's what she said."

"If she passes away while I am gone, it's okay. I have great memories of her, Grandpa, and Grandma Madge in my life. Those won't change. I don't feel like I have to make up for lost time."

"So you'd just skip the funeral?"

I paused. "Yes," I said. "At that point, she'd be gone."

He didn't like it, but Dad had to accept the fact that I was going to Europe, no matter what.

In the months and weeks that led up to the trip, I spent extra time with Grandma Millie. If she made it to a family party, I sat by her and listened or started the conversation and focused on her for awhile. A few days before I left, I went to her house. We talked for a while, and I told her the exciting details of my plans. When it was time to leave, I gave her a hug and a kiss and looked into her eyes.

> If you wait for the right moment, chances are, that time will never come.

"Grandma, this is goodbye. I love you," I said.

She patted my cheek. I leaned forward and kissed her cheek, and we hugged one more time.

"Be careful," she warned, and I left.

Grandma Millie was still here when I got back.

You can't live your life worried about what might happen. You have to seize your opportunities and leave unforeseen events to the future. I meet so many people who wait for all the conditions to be perfect, and I want to scream at them, "Quit waiting! Life will not wait for you; why wait for life?"

If you wait for the right moment, chances are, that time will never come.

EXCUSE BUSTER:

You might miss some things. So what? Make your dreams your priority!

Ask:

1. Why are you afraid of change?
2. What is the worst thing that could happen if you do this thing?
3. How would you handle those consequences?

Act:

1. Write down some of the major changes you've already experienced (e.g., graduated, went to a new school, moved to a new town, divorced parents, broke up with a boyfriend or girlfriend).
2. Write down the positive things that resulted from each of those changes.
3. Do you have a big dream that would require you to make a change? Examples: You want to try out for basketball, but none of your friends plays basketball. You want to try out for a play, but your

friends and family only care about sports. You want to go away to school, but it's far from home, and you don't know anyone there.

4. For your big dream, what is one change you'll have to make, in order to make it happen? Example. Spend less time with your non-sports friends to get in better shape and make that team; spend less time with your sports friends to get some experience for the play; move away to go to that faraway school, spend less time watching TV and more time on schoolwork, so you can get a scholarship.

5. In a perfect world, what would it take to make this change? Write down whatever comes to mind.

6. Be creative. Write down your plan to make it happen, and assume that everything will fall in your favor.

Excuse 10

It's Too Dangerous

When I told Dad I wanted to travel, one of the first things he said was, "The world is dangerous."

Is the world dangerous? Well, yes. Of course it is. But it's important to remember that *parts* of the world are dangerous. Just because dangerous places exist, doesn't mean that every place is dangerous.

Consider plane travel as an example. The 9/11 attacks crippled the airline industry for years because many people did not want to fly. Malaysian Airlines dealt with a double-whammy in 2014: the disappearance of Flight 370, and another plane that was shot down over Ukraine. We're tempted to use these examples to prove that flying is dangerous.

But research by Arnold Barnett, an M.I.T. professor, concluded that between 2009-2013, "the death risk for passengers in the United States has been one in 45 million flights. In other words, airplane travel has become so reliable that a traveler could fly every day for an average of 123,000 years before being in a fatal crash." On the other hand, the National Highway Traffic Safety Administration stated that in 2010, there were 32,885 deaths on U.S. highways.

The numbers suggest that travel by car is much more dangerous than air travel. Every few months, we may hear about a plane crash that killed hundreds of passengers. But we routinely tune out the thousands of stories about fatal car accidents. Yet, airplane crashes make a bigger impression because they are more unusual, and more dramatic.

If we're not careful, we can make assumptions and draw false conclusions that prevent us from taking action, when a closer look would prove something different altogether.

If we're not careful, we can make assumptions and draw false conclusions that prevent us from taking action, when a closer look would prove something different altogether.

Morocco and the magic carpet

During the third week of my solo-travel, I found myself in southern Spain, where I plotted my next move. A few days earlier, I had been on a train to Madrid and had shared a cabin with three Australian teenagers. Barry, Mark, and Alex had been counselors at a youth camp together and came to Europe before they started college. I told them my story, and we talked about going to Morocco, since we were so close to that country.

We made plans to meet up after a few days in Madrid, and to take on Morocco together. They would stay for camping and hiking, but I only planned to stay one day, and then I would go back to Europe.

"I just hope it's not dangerous," I told Barry.

"No worries, Mate, it won't be bad," he replied.

A few days later, the four of us survived an overnight train ride from Madrid to Algeciras, a coastal city on the southern tip of Spain. A morning ferry would take us across the Straits of Gibraltar to Morocco, and I'd get the much-desired passport stamp from Africa.

We got off to a rough start. Just like on an international flight, before boarding the ferry we had to go through customs, which caught us by surprise and took forever. The vessel, several times the size of a house, carried a small army of vehicles and passengers. The ride that was supposed to take just over an hour turned into a three-hour ordeal, as we navigated through extremely choppy waters. We sat in front of a thick window and watched the towering waves crash into the glass. The giant ship pitched up and down. I felt sick, but tried to act normal. My energy plummeted, and I started to feel dizzy.

"You don't look so good," said Barry. "You need to lie down?"

"Definitely. And I have to stop looking at these waves."

I relaxed away from the windows until the ferry pulled into the port of Tangiers. Another painful hour of customs ate up more time once we de-boarded the ferry. Instead of arriving at 10:00 a.m. with the whole day ahead of us, we got started around noon and had only a few hours to look around.

Somehow, my new friends and I were the last people to get off the ferry. A cacophony of voices hit us. All the wild-eyed, bellowing cab drivers and tour guides that had not gotten earlier customers swarmed us, their final hope for a fare that day.

"What on earth is this?" Barry leaned over and shouted to me.

"Let's pick a taxi and get out of here," I said.

We relented to one persistent guy and paid a small fee to this scowling, scruffy henchman who wore a dirty flannel shirt, jeans, and worker boots. No one felt good about it.

"Welcome to my country," he growled with a deep accent and a checkerboard smile.

He loaded our stuff into the back of his four-door car for a jaunt around the city, a "no strings attached" tour. A few minutes later, we stood on top of a four-story building and admired the panoramic view of the port. The buildings stretched before us like a table of tan Lego structures. The water now rested peacefully, with some mountains visible in the distance.

"Every year, people try to escape from Morocco, pay lots of money to get on boats, and take their chances with the crossing," our guide said.

"How does that turn out?" I asked.

"Sometimes they get turned around and end up back on our shores. They are so excited until someone comes up to them and says, 'Welcome to Morocco,'" the henchman said with some added chuckles.

He invited us below for some mint tea. Although a little confused with this "tour," the lack of any food or drink for several hours made us follow him down the stairs and through a sliding door.

"Take off your shoes, my friends," he said gruffly. "Put your backpacks over here."

We entered a maze covered in carpets. Every surface boasted intricate, detailed rugs that featured colorful, unique designs. We lingered around a low table in a side room, and a man entered the room with a tray of tea.

His name was Abdul. He had flattened black hair and a short mustache, and sported a flowing, royal blue robe. He was much cleaner and smoother than our tour guide, the henchman. He looked like he could have been on the Sultan's staff in the movie *Aladdin*.

"Please, my friends, sit down! Have some mint tea!" he exclaimed in English. He had perfect grammar and a slight Middle-Eastern accent.

He asked about our home countries and our education and shared some of his experiences as an exchange student in California.

"I love America! I made many friends there!" he said cheerfully.

As we finished the mediocre tea, I began to wonder why we were there. I had the same feeling as when the weather changes right before a big storm is coming. Almost to the second, Abdul made it clear. The henchman entered from some unseen room with a rolled-up carpet in his arms and laid it flat in front of us. Not only did the storm hit, but tornado sirens went off in my head. We were in the middle of a sales pitch. My defense mechanisms told me we needed to get out of there.

I grew up in a neighborhood that was racially mixed, but my high school was ninety-five percent white. At college, Loyola had a diverse population, but the different groups seemed mostly segregated. My experiences with diversity were very limited. My default impression of this Moroccan man, I'm ashamed to admit, was based on the Middle Eastern terrorists I'd seen in movies.

Manners told me to be polite and wait till Abdul gave us an opportunity to excuse ourselves. Manners won out. In fact, before I could do anything, Abdul escorted me—by myself—through several doorways, deeper into the building. He told me to wait. My heart raced as I took stock of this predicament. It felt dangerous.

I was alone, I was hungry, and I wasn't sure how I could get out of this building, let alone how to get around this city or country. No one in the world knew that I'd come to Morocco except for the three Australian strangers I met a couple of days ago. Above all, I didn't know where my shoes or bag were, and the carpets that surrounded me on all sides soaked up all the sound like a sponge.

I was trapped.

I could only envision the worst intentions of the Middle-Eastern bad guy in every action movie I had ever seen. I genuinely felt that I would be held at gunpoint if I did not buy a carpet.

Abdul proved to be excellent at reading people and the situation. He had assessed me to be the "rich American college student," traveling alone, and thought I was more likely to cave under pressure. The three younger Australian guys were "poor teenagers," less likely to spend money, harder to convince since they were in a group, and were not dependable sales prospects. Except for the "rich" part, he was dead on.

After waiting about twenty minutes, my captor approached me and started his pitch. He never made mention or motion, but I was convinced that he had a gun somewhere under that loose robe, and if I made any false move, he would pull it on me. I concentrated, stayed calm, and ignored the frequent growl from my stomach. My plan was to talk my way out of the situation.

"The only reasonable feeling anyone could possibly have toward this particular rug is love," he began.

He continued, and I nodded in agreement with almost everything he said. Until he got to the cost.

"The only reasonable amount for this creation is one thousand, six hundred."

"Dollars???!!!" I asked and exclaimed at the same time. I laughed.

He glared at me, turned, and walked out without a word. A few minutes passed before he came back.

"No way," I responded. "I don't have that kind of money for a rug."

"It is not just a rug," Abdul replied. He lowered his voice, and lay the accent on thick. "It is art."

The tension eased a little, and I focused on the negotiation instead of fearing for my life.

"Okay, my friend," he began again. "I like you. For sixteen hundred dollars, you can get two and sell one in America to cover the cost.

"I'm backpacking," I objected. "I can't carry these around Europe."

"You are young and strong," Abdul replied.

Now I was amused. This guy was good. On the outside, I smiled a bit, but inside I was still pretty worried. I wanted to get the heck out of there with my life intact and without the added weight of a Moroccan rug that lightened my wallet.

Abdul asked, I refused, the price dropped, and his lines kept getting better. The absolute best one came after he had lit up a cigarette.

"This is just too expensive," I emphasized.

"You will not think so," he said with a puff of smoke, "when you make love on it."

I became even more amused, but my nerves were too frayed for me to react. The end of the line felt near. At last, Abdul made a mistake.

"Here's what you can do, my friend," he said. "This piece is only $100. You will graduate next year. Give me your credit card number, and I won't charge you until you graduate, when you can get a job and pay me."

He thought I was still in school—I hadn't told him I had already graduated! His logic gave me plenty of time to get out of paying the $100, and in the meantime, I could get out of there alive.

"Let's do that," I said with a forced calm that hid my excitement.

Abdul's smiled and gave me a hug. "My friend!" he said with a huge grin.

The henchman came in, folded up the rug and tied it in plastic. He somehow compacted it so that it would fit in a brown paper grocery bag. I figured if I could get out of there, maybe I could ship it home later.

Abdul and the henchmen were all smiles.

"Please come again, my friend," he said with a wave.

I hustled out and ran into the three Aussie boys at a nearby cafe. At long last, I ordered something to eat. Then we shared what had happened the previous two hours.

"They got you to buy something?" Barry asked.

None of these three guys seemed fazed. I realized that Abdul had spent most of his time with me, not them. I now felt angry and embarrassed, yet massively relieved.

"Did you get anything?" I asked them. Together, they shook their heads no.

I refused to feel stupid. I was safe. At worst, I had lost a hundred dollars, but I still had my life.

We parted ways. They went into Morocco, and I headed back to the port, since the afternoon was gone. My only hope to get on the evening train to Seville was to catch the seven p.m. ferry. A map and some street signs pointed the way to the dock. My pack was a bit heavier because of the spectacular Moroccan rug I'd traded for my life.

JOE FINGERHUT

The henchman made one final appearance. He walked beside me on the last short stretch to the port.

"Go back to your country," he snarled with some English curse words mixed in there. I was, indeed, determined to get out of his country in one piece. He finally left me alone.

At long last, I boarded the ferry, and on an outside deck under the stars, I met a man from Aruba, who worked as a lawyer in the region. His name was Harro, and like so many people I had met on this trip, he went through cigarettes as often as most people check their watches.

"I thought my life was in danger!" I said breathlessly and told him all the details of my rug-buying episode.

He laughed. "Guns are illegal in Morocco," he said in between drags.

"What?!" I demanded.

"They don't want their people to shoot the king," he explained, which at this moment, made all the sense in the world. "Guns are illegal in most countries, my friend."

We talked for the rest of the three-hour ferry ride. An older couple from England sat near us, and when we got back to the port in Spain, they were going to drive their car to Marbella, a coastal town about three hours away. Coincidentally, Harro was headed there, as well, and they offered him a ride. The ferry finally arrived in Algeciras after midnight, long after the last train had left for Seville or anywhere else. The couple drove me to the train station, which was pitch black and all locked up.

"Why don't you come to Marbella with me, and we can get you on a train in the morning?" Harro volunteered, and the couple agreed.

"That would be incredible," I said with deep gratitude.

I squeezed into the back seat of their tiny European car, and joined three strangers on a midnight drive along the coast of the Mediterranean Sea. My head tilted to appreciate the brilliant night sky. The stars distracted me from the heavy weight of the overstuffed backpack I held on my lap. I nodded off and woke up when we reached a hotel in Marbella. Harro and I offered to pay the couple for the ride, but they refused, and we watched them drive away.

"I need to find a phone," I told Harro.

It was 3:30 a.m. in Spain—9:30 a.m. in St. Louis. I used a calling card and dialed my home number. Mom picked up.

"Is everything okay?" she asked.

"Absolutely. I need you to cancel my credit card. I'll explain later," I said firmly and got off the phone. I had escaped the financial death grip of Abdul, and I got away with his beautiful rug.

A few hours later, Harro put me on a train to Seville. As the train sped along, I pondered the unbelievable events that had happened since the previous morning. I had swung from fearing for my life based on the false assumption that I was in danger, to appreciating the kindness of strangers. I had a lot to learn.

That experience opened my eyes and taught me that the world is not like an action movie. I learned that the U.S. is, in fact, one of the few countries where guns are legal. That does not automatically make entire countries safe, but it is somewhat reassuring. Unless a particular destination lies in a war zone, there are plenty of areas that are safe to visit.

Disease in Vietnam

I had another break in the Japanese school year, and I wanted to go Vietnam. My brother was also living in Japan, and we were excited to experience a new country. Many people had told us about the beauty of Vietnam, the nice people, the bargains on everything, and the safe atmosphere. We were sold.

But in the months before our trip, a health scare had put Asia, and the world in general, on alert. The SARS epidemic started in China, and cases had been documented around Asia and other countries. Even though Vietnam itself had not been greatly affected, the proximity to China was a genuine concern. We had learned to practice due diligence, and some research played a key role in making our plans.

Our parents and some friends warned against going to Vietnam while SARS dominated the headlines. Some of our supervisors indicated they preferred we make other arrangements, too.

"I would really feel better if you boys did not go to Vietnam," Mom wrote in an email.

"So, about Vietnam," our Japanese supervisor said. "Maybe you should be careful." In his mind, he had directly told us not to go. But we only heard a light warning about our safety.

"Dude, you're crazy to go there right now!" a Canadian friend said.

We took our family and friends' feelings to heart but wanted to get a wider, more informed perspective.

The U.S. government issues travel advisories that cover issues from political instability and terrorism to natural disasters and threat of disease. At that time, a travel advisory advised Americans to steer clear of Vietnam.

A British friend gave us a tip. "Check the advisories for other countries," he said. "Sometimes America goes overboard."

"England is a little less sensitive about that stuff?" I asked.

"Something like that. If someplace is truly dangerous, America and England will have similar stances. It helps to get more than one view."

I found advisories for Vietnam from England, Canada, and Australia. As opposed to America's definite policy to stay out, the other advisories took a more informative, cautious tone. We took comfort in the fact that even though our home country didn't quite approve of travel to Vietnam, similar countries did not have a major problem with it.

We also consulted with the World Health Organization. The WHO monitors the status of conditions and provides assistance to affected areas around the world. Thankfully, around the time we had planned to go to Vietnam, the WHO issued an encouraging declaration.

"Did you see the news?" my brother said.

"No, I haven't seen anything," I told him.

"The WHO declared Vietnam to be a clean country. We are totally good to go!"

Despite the trepidation from our family, employers, and even our own government, we felt we had gathered enough facts to justify our trip, so we forged ahead. We got on the plane to Vietnam with a clear conscience and looked forward to the wonders that awaited us.

Vietnam is a third world country that has endured decades of military struggles, and it relies on the tourism business to support the economy. The SARS scare had driven most of the tourists away and had hurt them badly.

On our first day, we stopped in a couple of different hotels to compare their rates.

"They hardly have any guests," my brother said.

"You're right," I said. "All these places are giving us big discounts because they're excited to see us."

We ran across plenty of people from other countries, but we were often the only passengers on our day trips. We scored great deals on hostels and dinners, and because there were so few tourists, we built solid connections with the Vietnamese people.

One day, Mark and I hopped in a van for a day-long excursion of the Cu Chi tunnels in South Vietnam. These tunnels had played an important role in the Vietnam War. With only the guide and the driver with us, we journeyed through towering, lush bamboo forests. We passed bombed-out tanks that were still intact from the Vietnam War. We spent the afternoon crouching through long, narrow tunnels that wound around the countryside. Our guide, Nahm, told us that up to ten thousand people had lived in these tunnels. The Vietnamese had used the tunnels as an escape from, as well as a strategic tool for, the fighting at ground level. We spent the entire day with him and had access to a walking encyclopedia of the country.

If we had been part of a large throng of tourists, we wouldn't have made this deeper connection or gotten insight into Nahm's life and the outcome of the war.

"I didn't realize," I said, "that America lost the Vietnam War."

My brother agreed, and added, "I don't even remember being told that in school."

America, despite the recession of recent years, thrives as a world power, but Vietnam remains a developing nation. Nahm summed up the effects of the war.

"Sometimes you have to lose to win. And sometimes when you win, you really lose." I never forgot those words.

> "Sometimes you have to lose to win. And sometimes when you win, you really lose."

I'm glad that my brother and I had the opportunity to go to Vietnam and to experience what we did. But if we had listened to other voices, we would have missed it.

We will always have people in our lives who express doubt or discourage us from doing what we want to do. Their feelings may not be wrong, but they also might not be entirely right. It's our responsibility to explore all the aspects of a situation. Sometimes other people project their own fears and limitations onto us, and while we can recognize that their opinions are valid, we can draw our own conclusions by seeking information from multiple sources.

Mugged in Rio

My wife, Michiyo, and I arrived in Rio de Janeiro, Brazil, and checked into a hotel the first night of our honeymoon. We decided to head straight to Rio's main attraction.

"This is our first night in Brazil," I told the man at the desk. "We want to see the beach and the ocean."

"Don't go to the beach at night," he said. "Very dangerous."

"No problem," I said.

In my head, I thought he meant that we shouldn't go late at night, like eleven o'clock or midnight. Of course, his warning made sense in that context.

We walked a few blocks among the office buildings and hotels and enjoyed a pizza and drinks for dinner. Aside from street signs and the sounds of the Portuguese language, Rio seemed like any conventional city. After dinner, we crossed a busy boulevard called Avenue Atlantica. Copacabana Beach stretched out before us, introducing us to fifty miles of Brazilian beaches.

"We are officially in South America!" I gushed to Michiyo.

From the sidewalk, we couldn't see the ocean, although we could hear the waves crashing lightly in the distance. The sand stretched out forever and there was plenty of room for multiple volleyball courts, soccer fields, and several other sports that must have been local favorites. Tall poles topped with bright lights illuminated each section.

Between the crowds and the lights, it felt like midday, even though it was eight o'clock at night.

"I really want to step in the water," I said to Michiyo.

"Let's go!" she agreed.

We joined hands and carried our shoes and socks. As we walked further away from the bustle, the sounds of the water overtook the chatter of people. Our path was lit by the bright sand, since the lights stopped where the crowds gathered for sports. The closer to the water we got, the fewer people we saw. The beach followed a gradual slope down to the water, which was black in the darkness.

I'd had a few drinks and needed to relieve myself.

Off in the distance near the water, we noticed some joggers, and two of them seemed to be running toward me. I assumed they would be like the numerous strangers I had met before. I was certain these men would be happy to meet a foreigner, and the strangers would turn into friends.

The clean-shaven man in front was wearing navy blue soccer shorts, a yellow Brazilian soccer jersey, and a tan baseball hat. The bearded man behind him wore only a pair of red swimming trunks. Neither wore shoes. Their faces looked friendly enough.

"Hello!" I said with a happy smile and a big wave.

"Hello," the first man said in a deep voice, with his hand up, like a wave. But he did not smile.

When he closed the gap between us, I took a step backward to create some personal space. *Maybe Brazilian people like to talk up close*, I thought.

I took small steps backward in the sand and felt off balance for a moment. I was confused about why this man was getting so close to me, but understood completely when he put his hand on my chest and pushed me down.

I was in trouble.

Barefoot and seated in the sand, I panicked. He stood over me, and the second man caught up to us. They did not hurt me right away, but one of them searched through the pockets of my shorts with expertise. He had done this many times before.

I considered fighting my way out of this dilemma, but then I saw a knife in the right hand of the man who stood over me. My focus became to simply get away or get help. They could have whatever was in my pockets, but I would not just lie there and get hurt.

"Michiyo! Help!!!" I yelled as loud as I could.

"Hey, what are you doing? Get away!" Michiyo yelled. I saw her running toward us.

The two men darted away toward the water and up the beach.

I sat up, stunned, and Michiyo crouched next to me.

"Are you okay?" she asked, breathing hard.

"I think so," I said, as anger and adrenaline joined the flood of relief.

"We can't go after them," I said out loud.

"Of course not," said Michiyo. "What happened?"

"They came up and pushed me down. One of them had a knife."

"What? Let's get out of here."

We gathered our shoes and socks and hurried back to the well-lit area where the volleyball games continued with people smart enough not to go near the water at night. We sat down to catch our breath. By this time, embarrassment overtook my anger. I felt like everyone knew what had happened, and they all looked at the stupid American with amusement. In reality, no one knew what happened, and no one cared.

"I'm just glad you weren't hurt," said Michiyo. "What did they want?"

"I don't know," I said. Then I checked my pockets. "Oh, of course. My pocket is empty. They got the money."

"How much?"

"I'm not sure. But we had just cashed those Travelers Checks for about a hundred and fifty dollars."

We were both silent. Michiyo rubbed my back with one hand.

The whole episode lasted only a few minutes, but it cast a dark cloud over the first night of our honeymoon. We walked back to the hotel in a fully defensive mode. We looked around every corner and jumped at every noise. Once we settled in, we reviewed the situation.

"We didn't listen to the hotel guy," Michiyo said.

"You're right," I agreed. "He said 'don't go at night,' and I thought he meant late at night. But we went when it was dark. That's what he meant. We were wrong."

"So what do we do?"

"We have two options," I said. "We can give up and go home. Being robbed at knifepoint on our first night in Brazil could be a bad sign. Or we can be smarter about what we do and give ourselves a few days to calm down. Forget about the money and focus on enjoying ourselves."

We thought for a few moments.

"I don't want to go home," I said. "This could have happened anywhere."

"We just have to be smarter," Michiyo added.

We made it through the next week with no problem. Rio de Janeiro was our first stop, and other than being robbed by a man with a knife, we had a phenomenal time. People were polite, helpful, and happy to meet friendly foreigners, just like I expected.

EXCUSE BUSTER:

Too dangerous? Do your research, and if it makes sense, do it anyway!

Ask:

1. Do you think the world is dangerous? Why?
2. Are your assumptions based on fear or fact?

Act:

1. Do you want to travel? Write down some places you want to go, and include at least one foreign country.
2. If time and money were not a factor, what other fears are holding you back from going there? List them all (Example: lodging, language, transportation, safety).
3. Start a Google Search with the words, "_____ trip." Fill in the blank with your country.
4. Compile the information you find in one place (i.e., copy and paste info into one document or file folder).

5. Plan a virtual trip. No limits. Figure out what one week might look like in that country. How long is the flight? Where could you stay? What would you like to do? What would you like to eat?

6. Finally, answer this question: How soon can you take this trip?

Excuse 11

They Won't Like Me

There was something else that bothered my dad: People in other countries don't like Americans. Like so many other myths, this is simply a generalization, not a fact. While certain stereotypes may proceed us, whether people like us as individuals depends on our own humility, confidence, and the attitude we project.

According to an old folk tale, an old man sat outside the walls of a great city. When travelers approached, they would ask the old man, "What kind of people live in this city?" The old man would answer, "What kind of people live in the place where you came from?" If the travelers answered, "Only bad people live in the place where we came from," the old man would reply, "Continue on; you will find only bad people here."

> While certain stereotypes may proceed us, whether people like us as individuals depends on our own humility, confidence, and the attitude we project.

But if the travelers answered, "Good people live in the place where we came from," then the old man would say, "Enter, for here, too, you will find only good people."

When I started traveling, I had heard that being an American could be a disadvantage, a concern expressed by my friends and relatives, as well as some of the guidebooks I read. They said that Americans have a reputation for being arrogant and loud. To avoid this stereotype, some Americans even sewed Canadian flags on their backpacks because Canadians are generally better received.

I did not accept that stereotype. While I was in Europe, I adopted the attitude that I knew nothing. The places I went were not on my home turf, and the people I met were not responsible to cater to my needs. My goal was to get a view of other people, places, and cultures and to create a positive impression of Americans.

"Just be nice," said my friend who had studied in Italy. "If you are nice, the Italians will generally be nice."

"Easy enough," I said.

"They are very curious about Americans," he added.

A girl in my dorm had studied abroad and had traveled around Europe a bit. "Learn a few phrases in their language," she encouraged.

"Like which ones?" I asked.

"Instead of saying, 'Do you speak English?' begin with, 'I'm sorry, I don't speak your language so well.'"

"That makes sense. So you start of with an apology," I said.

"Yes, that helps. Especially in France. After that, learn how to say hello, excuse me, I'm sorry, and thank you."

At the hostel in Paris, I talked to a lot of other backpackers from different countries. "What is your impression of Americans?" I asked Andrew, a new friend from Denmark.

"I think the stereotype of the 'Ugly American' is true," he said.

"Tell me about that," I said politely.

"You know, loud and cocky. Think they know everything."

"Have you met a lot of people like that?" I asked.

"No," he said matter-of-factly. "All the Americans I've met have actually been pretty cool."

I got the same response from a number of people. Most Americans were different from what they expected. They were "different in a better way," but there were some exceptions.

"We were at this restaurant in Italy," a woman from Norway said, "and a man from New York was yelling at the servers and staff, saying things like, 'I'm from New York! You are nothing without us! We own you!'"

"I'm sorry that happened," I said, feeling embarrassed on behalf of Americans.

"He was a jerk, no matter where he came from," she concluded.

It was easy to see how one person who acted like that could erase all the good impressions a hundred other Americans created.

I decided I would learn a few greetings in each language and approach every situation as my opportunity to learn. And it worked. Several times, people complimented me for attempting to speak their language, and I can still see the look of appreciation on their faces because their words meant so much to me.

Gregory in France.

Lenka in the Czech Republic.

Johan from Sweden.

They each said a variation of the same thing: "I like you. You are not what I expected from an American."

My favorite comment was from a new acquaintance. He said, "I like you, but I don't like your government."

If you're going to travel internationally, you need to be prepared for comments like that. I always respond with, "Me too!" no matter how I feel, which makes that person an instant friend. If I agree with what they say, a healthy conversation and discussion often follows.

The bottom line is that people are people, no matter where they live. You don't like to be around people who think they know everything, and the same goes for everyone else. People want to be around kind, courteous, considerate people. If you keep that in mind, whether you're in America or somewhere else, you can help change that stereotype from "ugly" to "beautiful American."

In every country I visited, I tried to demonstrate a humble attitude and a hunger for knowledge. And I never put a Canadian flag on my backpack. As a result, I've developed friendships on every continent except Antarctica, only because I haven't been there—yet!

> People want to be around kind, courteous, considerate people.

NOT number one

In America, we do a pretty good job of building ourselves up as "the greatest country in the world." Our three holidays that define summer—Memorial Day, Fourth of July, and Labor Day—provide ample opportunity to celebrate America as the biggest and best. The Olympics are yet another stage where we demonstrate our national pride, and we usually earn impressive results. It's hard to grow up here and not have confidence and appreciation for America's history, accomplishments, and our prominent place in the world. I do love this country, even though it will never be perfect.

And how could anyone from another country NOT think that America is NUMBER ONE!!! I thought the facts were fairly straightforward. In a mere two hundred years, America has been victorious in not one, but two World Wars. America has been at the forefront of everything from culture to technology; We're the only ones who have professional football, and we are clearly the best at any sport that truly matters.

I was confident and proud that I had been born in a country that had been and would stay in first place, and I felt bad that people in other countries knew that they could never be better than second place.

These beliefs show how I used to think. But as I grew older, explored more places, and met more people, my perspective changed. I was forced to examine whether my beliefs were based on fact.

In a restaurant in Seoul, Korea, my American friend, Ed, and I experienced the spicy assault that is called Kim Chi. In Korea, this dish of seasoned cabbage made our noses sting, set our mouths on fire, and opened floodgates in our eyes. As we struggled to minimize the flames that shot from our heads—even after we inhaled rice and water to try to calm it down—a bespectacled, twenty-something Korean guy in a polo shirt and jeans approached us.

"You like Kim Chi?" he asked.

Ed and I, between fits of laughter and gulps of water, nodded yes, and Ed scooted over for our new friend to join us. He told us to call him Rick, which was his adopted English name.

"Where you from?" he asked.

"America," I said. "Ed is from Atlanta, and I am from St. Louis. Have you heard of those cities?"

"No. I been to New York," Rick shared.

"Cool!" said Ed. "What did you think about New York?"

Ken scrunched his face up and shrugged.

"Too big," he said. "How you like Korea?"

He asked the question just as Ed and I chomped on another mouthful of Kim Chi, and we reacted accordingly. But we acknowledged his question and gave an enthusiastic thumbs-up and smiled.

He followed up with, "How you like America?"

I recovered enough to answer. "It's great," I said. "My family is there, there's lots to do, we have everything we need. You know, we are in the greatest country in the world."

Our conversation had been simple up to that point, but this was our first exchange that was lost in translation.

Ken replied, "Yes, you are in Korea."

Confused, I said, "You think Korea is the greatest country in the world?"

With a smile Ken said, "Of course."

Our conversation continued, but I was stuck on the fact that he thought Korea was the best. It was a cataclysmic shift in perspective. OF COURSE this man did not think America was number one! Why would he? Korea was his home.

Just like that, the dominoes started to fall. In an instant, I realized that a lot of people probably feel pretty good about their home country, which explains a lot about why there have been so many struggles for power and superiority throughout history: My place is better than yours. OF COURSE!

For the first time, I questioned whether America really was the greatest country in the world, and I started to pay more attention to the problems we face and the obvious flaws in so many areas of our society. I also realized that no country is perfect, but that doesn't mean that we cannot love where we are from.

Rick gave me a newfound appreciation for nationalism. I had always and still remain interested in the source of passion and joy for people. My new perspective has helped me recognize that we all have something in common, and we all think that our own home is the best.

EXCUSE BUSTER:

Think they don't like Americans? Then make them like YOU!

Ask:

1. What attitudes do you have or what actions do you take to treat others with respect?
2. Are you cocky about your hometown/city/country?
3. How can you learn to appreciate other people and cultures who are different from you?
4. This chapter addressed the reaction foreigners might have to Americans. In what other situations might you fear that other people won't like you? How does that affect what you do or don't do?

Act:

1. Think of a time when someone said something about you that they thought was true, but was completely wrong. Write it down.
2. Think of a time when you said something about someone you thought to be true, but turned out to be completely wrong. Write it down.
3. Write down five actions you can take toward other people that can transform neutral or negative interactions into something positive and empowering.

I Don't Speak Their Language

Back to Dad. "You can't travel to Europe," he told me. "You don't speak the language!" He was right. Not knowing the language can feel like a barrier, but is it really?

You don't actually have to be fluent in a foreign language to communicate. I've heard that communication is 93% nonverbal and only 7% verbal. Most of our communication is transmitted through our tone of voice, gestures, and other factors. There's a lot more to it than words, although when dealing with foreign languages, the verbal part does play a major role. Communication, at its heart, is about people connecting, which can happen at a very basic level.

One of my proudest moments as a dad came when my son, Hiroki, learned to ride his bike without training wheels. We practiced for months. He had a yellow bike with Spider-Man designs all over it. He'd strap on his helmet and glide along with training wheels attached. He learned to speed up, slow down, and use the brakes to skid. One Sunday morning, he told me what he wanted to do that day.

> Communication, at its heart, is about people connecting, which can happen at a very basic level.

"Daddy," Hiroki said, "today I want to ride my bike without the training wheels."

"Are you sure?" I asked.

"Yes, let's do it!"

I removed his training wheels with just a bit of parental anxiety. This was a big step. At first, I kept my hand on his back while he pedaled, but he really didn't need that. For half an hour, we went up and down the sidewalk in front of our house. He pushed off and pedaled about three or four feet on his own, then put both feet down and started again.

"You're almost there!" I shouted several times.

The next day, we took his bike to my dad's house, which is on a cul-de-sac. Smooth pavement and no traffic made for the perfect place to ride without worries. We got out his bike and off he sped. Within seconds, he cruised the circle like he'd been doing it for months.

"Daddy, look! I can ride a bike!" he yelled.

My son had reached a basic level of competence. Although he was as far from the skills of professional BMX stunt rider as I was from being an astronaut, he had learned to ride a bike. And that minimum level of ability gave him something in common with other riders who'd reached the highest level of that activity.

When language is an obstacle, communication is like learning to ride a bike. If you have a very basic level from which to function, you might not be ready to compete at the highest level, but the minimum level will take you a long way. If you make the effort to learn some basics, it makes all the difference.

The most beautiful word

A person's name is the sweetest sound in the world to them. When you remember someone's name, it opens doors. And learning a little bit about what defines them, such as their language, ranks right up there with knowing their name. When you appreciate others, they open their hearts with ease, and open hearts lead to helpful, rich connections.

> When you appreciate others, they open their hearts with ease, and open hearts lead to helpful, rich connections.

So what do you do? In addition to learning a few basic phrases in other languages, prepare your attitude before you enter a new country. Tourism drives the economy in so many countries, and many travelers focus only on themselves: they are on vacation, they don't want to think, they want to be served, and they demand good service. The people who provide these services are often marginalized or viewed as nonpersons, like they're part of the scenery. If you show respect for their culture and their language, they will welcome you as a guest and offer genuine smiles and appreciation, rather than forced courtesy.

Navigating Cairo

Of course, language is much more than a device for good will. If you get lost or frustrated when you can't figure out how to do something or find an answer, language is an effective tool.

During our honeymoon, my wife and I boarded a plane to Egypt after we'd spent a few weeks in Turkey. We'd planned to spend almost two weeks visiting the Pyramids in Giza and several other historic places. This was our first experience traveling in Muslim countries. We had heard that our English would be sufficient in most areas and that Arabic was nearly impossible to learn. However, on the plane, we decided to challenge ourselves.

"Let's see if we can learn some Arabic," Michiyo said.

"Get out the guidebook," I said. "The basic words should be in there." We studied the pronunciation of thank you, which sounds like "Show-Caron."

"Check out the numbers," I said. "They seem to be pretty simple."

"I see a few patterns here," Michiyo noticed. "One, two, and three look like each other."

"Seven and eight are similar too," I added.

The other numbers seemed pretty easy. We didn't worry about pronunciation, but we practiced how to write all of them.

"All right, quiz me!" I said a few minutes later.

We tested each other for a while. One of us told the other to write down a specific number. Then we opened a magazine and looked for numbers to identify. We totally enjoyed the process.

"These might come in handy," I said.

In this case, those exercises served us well right off the bat. We cleared customs and picked up our bags in the airport outside Cairo, around five p.m. The airport was on the outskirts of the city, in a sea of endless sand. The heat slammed into us the moment we stepped out of the terminal.

"It's going to be hot at night," Michiyo said.

"Totally," I said. "Let's find a ride downtown and get a place to stay."

"We could just get a taxi," said Michiyo, without much conviction.

We had grown accustomed to the backpacker's challenge: figure out the cheapest alternative, even in the face of common sense. A safe, dependable taxi ride to downtown Cairo would not cost much. However, there was always the possibility of a lower-cost bus ride, plus the potential for a unique thrill in our first few hours in Egypt. It was too tantalizing to pass up. All we had to do was find the bus station.

We arrived during Ramadan, the Islamic month of fasting. Many people stayed indoors and adhered to a food fast till the bells rang near dark, when they all came out to enjoy dinner. There was only one person in sight—a tall Egyptian man with black hair and a thin beard, who wore a long, brown robe. He was smoking a cigarette and approached us slowly.

"You need taxi?" he asked in a low, dry voice with a Middle-Eastern accent. We were pleased that he spoke English.

"We want to take a bus," I replied. "Do you know where we can catch one?"

He leaned against the wall, lit another cigarette, took a drag, and looked straight ahead. "Bus station's closed. About thirty minutes ago."

We had backpacked in poorer countries before, where residents occasionally take advantage of inexperienced tourists, especially when no one else is around. I decided to push back a little bit.

"Even though it's closed, where is the building?" I repeated. He pointed at a building about a quarter mile away.

"I give you nice price for taxi," he said, but I shook my head, thanked him, and we started walking.

A few minutes later, we came to a small brick building in the middle of the parking lot, which was the bus terminal. All the signs were written with Arabic numbers, and I thought about going back to grab the taxi after all, but Michiyo checked the guidebook, which told us what bus number to take downtown.

"Check this out," she told me. "Number 342 should have rides for only two dollars!"

"Let's find 342," I said eagerly.

We reviewed the list of numbers we had studied on the plane, and picked out a spot to keep watch.

"This place is awfully quiet," Michiyo said. After fifteen minutes, there had only been a handful of busses that rolled in and out. We started to get a little nervous. Evening approached, and it was getting dark.

After an uneventful half hour passed, a long, dirty bus arrived. It had a white sign above the big windshield that was written in Arabic. I focused on the combination of numbers and was surprised that they made sense to me.

"Michiyo, can you look at that bus?" I said. "I am pretty sure that is 342, but could you confirm?"

Michiyo flipped to the guidebook, and looked back at the bus again.

"That should be it," she said.

"Wait here with our bags," I told her. "I'll see if we can take that one."

I walked to the bus, and the doors opened. My English came out simple and slow, just to make sure the driver understood me.

"Do you go into Cairo?" I asked the driver, a bald Egyptian man with a thick mustache and a white, button-down shirt.

"Yes, downtown is two dollars," he said, but then shook his head. "I can't take you."

"Why not?" I asked.

"I can't take just one rider," he said, and lifted his arm to motion to the empty seats.

My face lit up. "No problem! My wife is coming, too!"

He smirked and rolled his eyes. "Can't take just two. Sorry."

I paused, then had an idea. "What if I pay for four riders?"

That sealed the deal. He accepted eight dollars to give us a two-person, empty bus ride to Cairo. We may have overpaid, but neither of us cared. We set our bags down on the empty seats, stretched out, and took in the scenery on our one-hour, private journey into Cairo.

We scored a great deal and had a fun adventure because we had studied some numbers on the airplane. Our time in Egypt had started off with a success!

Japan: the first day of school

Before life in Japan, I knew as much Japanese as most Americans. The handful of words I knew were the names of brands, cities, foods, and random concepts, like Mitsubishi, Toyota, Honda, Nintendo. Cities like Tokyo, Nagasaki, Hiroshima, Okinawa. Foods such as sushi, teriyaki, and sake (the alcohol). And I knew a few other words like tsunami and sumo.

One of the biggest draws of the JET Program was that I didn't have to know Japanese. They simply wanted college graduates who spoke English. However, I was somewhat intimidated about being in a country where I couldn't read, write, or speak the language.

People still ask me, "How did you teach English if you couldn't speak Japanese?"

The short answer is: you don't. The JET Program was intended to expose Japanese students to people of other cultures. Teaching English is what brought us there, but no government directive dictated that the students needed to be fluent by the end of the school year. We just needed to do our best and be ourselves. It took me awhile to figure this out, but I learned how important it was to be myself on my first day of work.

When the alarm sounded on that first morning, my heart pounded with anticipation about what my life would be like for the next year. I'd spent a few weeks in the orientation program with other foreigners doing activities that helped us get settled. Now I would finally start my job as an English teacher.

It was important to make a good impression. I wore a simple gray business suit, and even though I would have to remove them at the front door of the school, I put on decent dress shoes to complete my look. These were the shoes I'd worn while training salespeople in America.

Now these shoes would pedal a bike and carry me to my new Japanese school in style.

I was only two steps outside, when the humidity hit me full force. Right away, a thin layer of sweat formed under my suit. I rolled up my right pant leg so the grease from the bicycle chain would not stain my best work clothes.

No turning back now, I thought, and eased onto the bike. Just as I started pedaling, some light raindrops hit my head and shoulders. *No big deal*, I thought. *It will just drizzle a bit, then stop. I'm sure it's just like St. Louis.* I figured I could tolerate a few minutes of drizzle, plus it might provide a little relief from the heat.

Within a few seconds, the sprinkles erupted into a thorough, torrential downpour. Rain seeped through every stitch of my suit. Halfway to school, I pedaled on, determined to overcome this temporary obstacle. Minutes could not be spared if I wanted to be on time for my first day. As quick and heavy as it began, the rain cleared up in an instant. The sun came out and radiated its heat over every soaked surface, which gave rise, again, to the breath-sucking humidity. My drenched suit weighed on me, but I couldn't help but smile at the ridiculousness of the situation. I was on a bike, in a full suit, in southern Japan, on my way to teach people English without knowing any Japanese. I was completely soaked, from my jacket down to my socks.

And then I arrived. I parked my bike, walked into the foyer, removed my shoes, and found some guest slippers. I coaxed my feet into the tiny blue, plastic slippers and walked toward the busy room. Lots of adults buzzed around, so I assumed this was the teachers' room.

The door slid open with a hiss, and when it did, all activity in the room stopped. Every eye went straight to the American wearing a sheepish smile and a soaked suit. I ached to explain how sorry I was, but the typical Japanese hospitality went into full force before I could utter one word. Several men and women surrounded me. One brought me a towel, another brought tea, and someone else took my jacket and hung it up to dry out.

The principal, Mr. Kinoshita, looked to be about my parents' age. His crisp, navy blue suit complimented his silver hair and wire-rim glasses.

"Joe sensei, you must be tired," he said with accented English. "Please, have some tea."

With a smile, a bow, and an uncomfortable nod, he motioned for me to sit, then walked to his own desk. I sipped some warm green tea and absorbed the hectic chaos of this first school day. One or two of the teachers introduced themselves to me, and these brief introductions showed me that their limited English skills matched my own level of the Japanese language. Polite smiles and nods from other teachers gave me a loose sense of welcome.

Bells rang, classes started, and the teachers came and went with each period. In the break between classes, students wandered in and out, tickled to get a glimpse of the new foreign teacher. "Hello, Hello!" they shouted with huge smiles, big waves, and giddy laughter. After a few hours, no teachers remained in the room. No sounds, footsteps, or voices lingered in the hallways. I was alone at an empty desk.

"Odd," I thought.

Then I heard a voice right next to my ear. It was Mrs. Ogawa, my teaching partner, and she spoke perfect English. Her voice was sweet and soothing.

"Joe sensei, now we will go to the gym," she said gently, giving me the most polite command she could.

"Great," I said, glad to be able to do something. "Is there a basketball game or something?"

She replied very matter-of-factly, "You will give your self-introduction."

I looked at her and waited for more information. She motioned for me to follow. I grabbed my jacket, which had dried out by now, and walked behind her. At the entrance to the gym, I saw some shelves filled with slippers. Everyone inside was wearing only their socks, so I added my own slippers to the pile.

We stood at the back of the gym and looked across the long basketball court toward the stage, where the assistant principal spoke into a microphone. Between us, there were four hundred students sitting on their knees in the Japanese style called 'seiza.' They were a stationary mass of silent seventh, eighth, and ninth graders, and they were all looking down at the floor in front of them. All I could see were their identical dark blue uniform jackets and the black hair on the back of each head. The gym windows were thrown wide open in defiance of the humidity. With so many people packed in one place, I felt like I could reach out and grab the thick air.

I listened to the assistant principal's words, but they sounded made up. Both the tone of his voice and his gestures made him seemed angry, particularly when he pointed a forceful finger at some of the students. In the middle of one of his sentences, the entire energy in the room changed when he added the English words "Joe Fingerhut sensei."

The students turned as one organism and, as odd as it sounds, it reminded me of the thick carpet in my aunt's basement. As kids, we used to rub our hands from one spot to another and watch the colors change. Just like that carpet, every head went from dark to light, as their black hair changed to reveal light-skinned faces with curious smiles. The entire mob split itself down the middle to form an aisle that ended at my feet, which were frozen in place. I gave a nervous smile as my stomach churned. What next?

"Joe sensei, now you can go and speak," Mrs. Ogawa said.

It was one of the hardest walks of my life. The room was silent as I shuffled along in socks. I kept telling myself, *Remember to smile. Put your right foot in front of your left and keep going.*

At the microphone, I faced this new community, and pondered what to say. I HAD NO JAPANESE WORDS!!!

Keep it simple, I thought to myself. *Think back to your public speaking. Start with a joke or a story.*

My mind flashed to a restaurant I'd seen a few days earlier. It had a sign in English that looked familiar: Ringerhut. Halfway around the world, in a country with a language nowhere close to English, there was a restaurant with a name that was only one letter off from my last name.

I began with a question. "Who likes Ringerhut?" I asked with raised eyebrows and an exaggerated smile.

I raised one arm to show the students what I hoped they would do. No one moved or spoke. Okay, plan B: find out if we had any common ground.

"Raise your hand," I said slowly, "if you can speak or understand even a little bit of English."

Same result. Not a muscle moved. *What do they want?* I thought.

I was neither a comedian, nor a Japanese speaker. I could only be myself and nothing more. That is all they expected. I took a breath, and spoke again.

"My name is Joe Fingerhut," I began with a slow, comfortable speed. "I am from St. Louis, Missouri, in America. I like basketball and baseball, and I love the St. Louis Cardinals. I am happy to be your English teacher. I look forward to meeting you."

My chin dipped, and I curled into a deep bow. The gym erupted in applause. All they had wanted was a few sentences spoken from my heart.

That moment in the gym was not about the language. It was about introducing a prominent new person to the community. They expected to simply see me for who I was, and they responded with joy once they saw it.

EXCUSE BUSTER:

There is more than one way to communicate! Take a risk and go anyway. The language will sort itself out.

Ask:

1. How do you approach new situations—with negative judgment or with an open mind?
2. What steps can you take to handle basic communication in another language?

Action Items:

1. Name a time when language—either a foreign language or a conversation you simply couldn't keep up with—held you back from connecting with someone.
2. What two steps could you take if you're in a similar situation in the future that could turn it into positive experience?
3. How can you communicate with your smile? With your body language? With your eyes?

Epilogue

Permission to be Proud

My cousin, David, and I had arrived at the Georgia International Convention Center in Atlanta. We walked the hallways, which were designed to handle huge crowds of people. Someone pointed us to the ballroom, where the opening session of the weekend conference would begin in a few hours.

The ballroom doors opened, and beyond the stage were three thousand empty chairs.

When I was in college, I had heard the motivational speaker Patrick Combs, who spoke to about one hundred students that day, including me. That's when I learned that a person could become a professional speaker. More importantly, I learned that there was at least one way to make a living by doing something fun while serving other people.

That's what I wanted, but I had all the typical excuses for not following that dream: I was too young. I didn't have any experience. Mom and Dad wanted me to do something else. I didn't have enough money. I didn't have enough time. I had other things to do. It might be dangerous. I didn't know anyone else who had done that. And on and on.

I always had other work opportunities, but my dream of becoming a public speaker stuck with me. Even while I backpacked across Europe, explored sales and marketing jobs, and taught English in Japan, my vision of being on stage remained vivid. I got married, learned how to be an entertainer, and after a decade of thought and a lot of preparation, I finally took action to become a professional speaker.

My path was never clear, but that ultimate goal was like a star that guided a caravan through the night. I wanted to be on stage and felt like I could make a career out of speaking. I never felt completely comfortable or qualified, but other people could never tell.

After several years of persistent action, I mustered up my nerve and called the director of a nationally known teen leadership program, and I introduced myself on her voice mail. A day later, she sent me an email.

"We looked at your materials," the email said, "and would like you to be our conference's opening keynote speaker."

She later told me that there would be over three thousand students and staff in attendance. I floated along in state of disbelief. Was this real? Could I handle it? In the weeks and days before the conference, I sought advice from other speakers, including Patrick Combs himself.

"You're gonna crush it!" he encouraged me.

David and I went to the ballroom for the afternoon sound check. He held the door open, I walked inside, and it took my breath away. I had no idea what this setting would look like. The atmosphere was much bigger than I had ever imagined. My knees went weak, and I crouched down for a minute to let the reality sink in.

The rows of chairs stretched forever and covered a floor the size of a football field. The aisles separated hundreds of chairs into neat sections. At the front of the room, red and blue lights illuminated a wide stage with two podiums at the outer corners. Dark curtains stretched from the edges of the stage to the wall and featured two large screens that would magnify the on-stage activities. This was big time!

We met the tech team, and they fitted a thin, flesh-colored microphone over my ear for a quick sound check. I stood at the center of the stage, gazed out at the sea of empty chairs, and visualized that room full of eager young faces. Every ounce of doubt and every sliver of second-guesses I had about myself vanished into thin air.

A few hours later, I stood alone backstage. Music poured into the ballroom as thousands of teen leaders flooded the aisles and filled the seats. I closed my eyes, took a breath, and smiled.

My dream had come true! The journey had not been easy, but I had stuck with it. I thought back to the first step, the first time I spoke in front of a group. *It all started with a phone call.*

I was scheduled to perform a magic show at a grade school for their two hundred students. Well into my career as an entertainer, I felt confident before a crowd like that. However, I wanted to become a speaker, and two conference planners from the NCADA (National Council on Alcoholism and Drug Abuse) had asked if they could evaluate me in person. I had to make something happen, so they could see me in action. My mom had once taught for this principal, so he knew me when I called him.

"Hi Joe, what can I do for you?" he asked.

"Rick, I'm giving your students a magic show this week," I began. "I want to ask you a favor."

"Name it, Joe."

"I ultimately want to work with students as a motivational speaker. Would you mind if I came about forty-five minutes early to speak to just the sixth, seventh, and eighth grade students?"

"I don't see why not. I'll clear it with the teachers and let you know."

That was my first official speech. I simply made a phone call and asked for exactly what I wanted. The NCADA planners showed up and were impressed enough to invite me to have a small role in their Prevention Leadership Conference. The next year, they hired me to be the keynote speaker. I had come a long way from that first opportunity. *It all started with a phone call.* A phone call—a simple first step.

Backstage in Atlanta, the microphone hugged my cheek. The event was being streamed live and my family, including my proud parents, had gathered back home in St. Louis to watch me take the stage. I reached down and turned on the receiver that was clipped to my belt. The voice of the host boomed through the speakers.

It all started with a phone call. A phone call—a simple first step.

"Our speaker tonight has lived, worked, and traveled in thirty countries on six continents. He has entertained and inspired thousands of people across America and around the world.

"Please welcome our keynote speaker, Joe Fingerhut!"

PART III

EXERCISES FOR INDIVIDUAL OR GROUP STUDY

Start NOW!

How Teens Can Build a Life
That is Fun, Fulfilling, and Promising

While Joe's story is entertaining and inspirational, the purpose of this book is give you the confidence to seize opportunities in your own life, try new things, and take risks. These efforts will require some targeted thought and a quite a bit of action on your part. If you want to build an extraordinary adult life that is fun, fulfilling, and promising, start NOW! You have to do the work to get you where you want to be.

Some teens can read the Excuse Busters at the end of each chapter and work through the questions and action items on their own to design their future lives. But most find it beneficial to work in groups, to bounce their ideas off others, and to hold each other accountable to the commitments and action items. This process works well for youth groups, leadership groups, and leadership seminars, but also for informal groups of two to three teens.

The following pages list the common excuses we have for not pursuing our dreams and specific exercises to work through to overcome those excuses. Don't shortchange yourself! Don't let anything stand in your way of a life that is fun, fulfilling, and promising. Give yourself permission to play!

Excuse 1

I Don't Know What I Want To Do With My Life

EXCUSE BUSTER:

Embrace the dream you hold in your heart and create an initial plan to pursue it!

Ask:

1. Write down several skills or jobs you'd like to explore. You aren't committed to DO them or master them at this point. The goal is to learn more about them.

    _____

    _____

    _____

2. Who can you talk to about this to learn more?

    _____

    _____

    _____

3. How can other people help you discover what your dream job might be?

    _____

    _____

    _____

4. Name something you want to do that is so important to you that you could ditch the fear of being ridiculed or being scolded and tell someone. Who will you tell?

_____

_____

_____

5. Picture your dream life. What kind of work would it include? What kind of activities or tasks would be involved? Write them down.

_____

_____

_____

6. Now write down the kind of activities or tasks you do NOT want in your life.

_____

_____

_____

7. How can you incorporate the things you love into your work, while avoiding the things you don't like?

_____

_____

_____

8. How have other people done this? Who inspires you?

Act:

1. Make a list of steps you can take that will put you on the path to a job that will be support your dream life.

_____

_____

_____

2. Pick one and DO IT!

_____

_____

_____

Excuse 2

My Parents Want Me To Do Something Different

EXCUSE BUSTER:

Try a new approach! Identify your desires, share them with your parents, don't worry about getting their approval at first, and ask them about their experiences.

Ask:

1. When have your parents disagreed with you about something you wanted to do?

   _____

   _____

   _____

2. How did you handle that?

   _____

   _____

   _____

3. What was the outcome?

   _____

   _____

   _____

4. In the end, did they ultimately agree or disagree with you?

_____

_____

_____

5. Could you see and appreciate their point of view?

_____

_____

_____

6. What steps did you take to consider things from their perspective?

_____

_____

_____

7. Do you feel like they tried to see things from your perspective?

_____

_____

_____

8. How much do you know about your parents' history?

_____

_____

_____

9. What jobs have they had?

_____

_____

_____

10. How did they meet?

_____

_____

_____

11. Why did they make the particular decisions they made about school, job, spouse, etc?

_____

_____

_____

12. Name some things that you want to do that is NOT on your parents' list of life experiences.

_____

_____

_____

13. How are your parents' expectations, or your even own beliefs, holding you back?

_____

_____

_____

Act:

1. Initiate a conversation with one or both of your parents. Start with, "What was life like for you at my age?"

_____

_____

_____

2. What did you learn that you didn't know before?

_____

_____

_____

Excuse 3

I Don't Have Enough Money

EXCUSE BUSTER:

Get real about money! Analyze how much you have, how much you spend, and how much you save, then make a plan to go after what you want.

Ask:

1. Think about your approach to pursuing opportunities and achieving goals. What are your negative or limiting thoughts?

_____

_____

_____

2. Is there something you'd would do if money weren't an issue? What is it?

_____

_____

_____

3. How do you feel about making a budget?

_____

_____

_____

Act:

1. Make a list of the fixed expenses in your life, if you have any.

   _____

   _____

   _____

2. Make a list of your fixed revenue (wages, other income).

   _____

   _____

   _____

3. Write down ways you can reduce your expenses.

   _____

   _____

   _____

4. Pick one crazy idea that you think is out of your financial league. Write it down as if it is already happening. For example, "I am studying abroad this summer," "I am attending Yale University next year," or "I have an internship in New York City this semester."

   _____

   _____

   _____

5. How much would that cost? Write it down. If you don't know, research it to come up with a loose figure.

   _____

   _____

   _____

6. How long will it take to make that idea a reality?

   _____

   _____

   _____

7. What are three changes you can make right now (either in spending habits, job position, the company you keep, etc.) that would reduce that amount of time? Pick one of them and start doing it NOW.

    _____

    _____

    _____

8. For one day, add the word YET to every sentence when you talk about the things you lack.

    _____

    _____

    _____

Excuse 4

This Isn't The Right Time

EXCUSE BUSTER:

Get moving! Pick something you want to do and take action toward that.

Ask:

1. Do you feel stuck on your current path?
   _____
   _____
   _____

2. Will your future self be happy if you continue on this path? Why or why not?
   _____
   _____
   _____

3. Is there something you enjoy doing but don't see how it relates to a future career?
   _____
   _____
   _____

4. Develop an end goal. Picture yourself ten years in the future, having achieved that goal. What did you do to make that happen? How did you break the cycle that had you trapped?

_____

_____

_____

Act:

1. Make a list of everything you are involved in and all of your commitments.

_____

_____

_____

2. Mark each entry with either "H" or "W." (H = have to be involved, W = want to be involved)

_____

_____

_____

3. For the H's, write down those reasons why you HAVE to be there.

_____

_____

_____

4. For the W's, write down how these activities may lead you to discover something else.

_____

_____

_____

5. Talk about your end goal with an advisor, a parent, or some other family member or friend who can be your a mentor. Write down

two or three steps you can take over the next three or four months that will put you on the path to that goal.

_____

_____

_____

6. This week, tell five people about your goal.

_____

_____

_____

Excuse 5

I'm Too Busy

EXCUSE BUSTER:

Think you're too busy? Get real about time and use it to your advantage!

Ask:

1. Do you feel bogged down by all the little things you have to do?

   _____

   _____

   _____

2. For your main goal, are you trying to do everything at once? Do you have a plan?

   _____

   _____

   _____

Act:

1. Keep track of your time in fifteen-minute increments for one week. Write it down!

   _____

   _____

   _____

2. At the end of the week, answer these questions: What were you most proud of? Where could you improve?

_____

_____

_____

3. Keep track of time in fifteen-minute increments for one more week. Review your previous week's notes. How did you improve? Which action made the biggest difference, and what will you continue to do moving forward?

_____

_____

_____

I Don't Have The Experience

EXCUSE BUSTER:

No experience? No problem—do it anyway!

Ask:

1. How is your lack of experience holding you back from pursuing something you'd like to do?
    _____
    _____
    _____

2. How often do you share your big goal or dream with people in your life?
    _____
    _____
    _____

3. Where can you volunteer that allows you to do that exact thing you want to do, even if you don't get paid for it?
    _____
    _____
    _____

4. Do you find reasons to say "no" to things instead of "yes?" What are those reasons?

_____

_____

_____

Act:

1. Write down one of your aspirations or goals. Examples: Is there a team you want to make? A school club you want to join (theatre/band/newspaper)? A certain college you want to attend? A part-time job you want?

_____

_____

_____

2. List one resource, person, or organization that could help you achieve that goal. Examples: Head/Assistant Coach, Advisor, Admissions office, Application Manager.

_____

_____

_____

3. This week, contact that person either by phone, email, snail mail, social media, or all of these methods. Tell them what you want to do, and ask what you can do to help THEM.

_____

_____

_____

Excuse 7

I Don't Know Anyone Else Who Has Done This

EXCUSE BUSTER:

Don't know anyone? Get out there and meet people, connect, and network!

Ask:

1. Are you drowning in ideas of things you should do but feel overwhelmed and can't pick one to start?

_____

_____

_____

2. What do you WANT to do?

_____

_____

_____

3. Name a family member or friend who has done it.

_____

_____

_____

4. If you don't have any family members or friends who have done it, what are some other ways you could connect with people who have that experience?

_____

_____

_____

5. Name some areas where you could ACT more confident?

_____

_____

_____

6. How does your uncertainty make you appear less competent?

_____

_____

_____

Act:

1. Write down the name of one person (they can be a celebrity, but they must be living), who does the kind of work you'd like to do.

_____

_____

_____

2. Do everything you can to find their contact information: phone, address, email, or social media information. Reach out to them through one of these methods.

_____

_____

_____

3. Keep your communication short. Tell them what you want to know, and be sincere. Example: "I'm a fan. I would love to do what you do. How did you get started?"

_____

_____

_____

4. Wait a week. If you don't get a response, identify another person and repeat this process.

_____

_____

_____

Excuse 8

I Can't Do This. It's Too Hard!

EXCUSE BUSTER:

You can do it! Take a positive look at yourself, and use your track record to give yourself credit for who you are and what you've already done!

Ask:

1. Are you trying to do too many things at once?

   _____
   _____
   _____

2. What does your resistance voice tell you?

   _____
   _____
   _____

3. Do you doubt yourself? Why?

   _____
   _____
   _____

Act:

1. Make a list of your personal victories. Start by writing down five of your achievements in the last five years, then expand your list to include more of your accomplishments. Give yourself credit for what you've done!

_____

_____

_____

2. Use a pen and paper to make two lists. On the first list, write down the most common things you hear your resistance voice say (Example: I'm not tall enough, good looking enough, cool enough, etc.). On the second list, write down the opposite statements.

_____

_____

_____

3. Cross out every line in the first list. Rip it up and throw it away.

_____

_____

_____

4. For one week, read your second list out loud in front of a mirror, twice a day—once when you get up and once before bed.

_____

_____

_____

5. For the entire week, you may not say ANYTHING to criticize yourself (Example: "I'm an idiot," "I am a slob," "I am not good looking"). Find positive alternatives to speak out loud, or don't say anything at all.

_____

_____

_____

6. At the end of the week, write down how you feel about yourself. Has there been any change?

_____

_____

_____

If I Do This, I'll Miss Out On Something Else

EXCUSE BUSTER:

You might miss some things. So what? Make your dreams your priority!

Ask:

1. Why are you afraid of change?

   _____

   _____

   _____

2. What is the worst thing that could happen if you do this thing?

   _____

   _____

   _____

3. How would you handle those consequences?

   _____

   _____

   _____

Act:

1. Write down some of the major changes you've already experienced (e.g., graduated, went to a new school, moved to a new town, divorced parents, broke up with a boyfriend or girlfriend).

    _____

    _____

    _____

2. Write down the positive things that resulted from each of those changes.

    _____

    _____

    _____

3. Do you have a big dream that would require you to make a change? Examples: You want to try out for basketball, but none of your friends plays basketball. You want to try out for a play, but your friends and family only care about sports. You want to go away to school, but it's far from home, and you don't know anyone there.

    _____

    _____

    _____

4. For your big dream, what is one change you'll have to make, in order to make it happen? Example: Spend less time with your non-sports friends to get in better shape and make that team; spend less time with your sports friends to get some experience for the play; move away to go to that faraway school, spend less time watching TV and more time on schoolwork, so you can get a scholarship.

    _____

    _____

    _____

5. In a perfect world, what would it take to make this change? Write down whatever comes to mind.

_____

_____

_____

6. Be creative. Write down your plan to make it happen, and assume that everything will fall in your favor.

_____

_____

_____

Excuse 10

It's Too Dangerous

EXCUSE BUSTER:

Too dangerous? Do your research, and if it makes sense, do it anyway!

Ask:

1. Do you think the world is dangerous? Why?

_____

_____

_____

2. Are your assumptions based on fear or fact?

_____

_____

_____

Act:

1. Do you want to travel? Write down some places you want to go, and include at least one foreign country.

_____

_____

_____

2. If time and money were not a factor, what other fears are holding you back from going there? List them all (Example: lodging, language, transportation, safety).

_____

_____

_____

3. Start a Google Search with the words, "_____ trip." Fill in the blank with your country.

_____

_____

_____

4. Compile the information you find in one place (i.e., copy and paste info into one document or file folder).

_____

_____

_____

5. Plan a virtual trip. No limits. Figure out what one week might look like in that country. How long is the flight? Where could you stay? What would you like to do? What would you like to eat?

_____

_____

_____

6. Finally, answer this question: How soon can you take this trip?

_____

_____

_____

Excuse 11

They Won't Like Me

EXCUSE BUSTER:

Think they don't like Americans? Then make them like YOU!

Ask:

1. What attitudes do you have or what actions do you take to treat others with respect?

   _____

   _____

   _____

2. Are you cocky about your hometown/city/country?

   _____

   _____

   _____

3. How can you learn to appreciate other people and cultures who are different from you?

   _____

   _____

   _____

4. This chapter addressed the reaction foreigners might have to Americans. In what other situations might you fear that other people won't like you? How does that affect what you do or don't do?

_____

_____

_____

Act:

1. Think of a time when someone said something about you that they thought was true, but was completely wrong. Write it down.

_____

_____

_____

2. Think of a time when you said something about someone you thought to be true, but turned out to be completely wrong. Write it down.

_____

_____

_____

3. Write down five actions you can take toward other people that can transform neutral or negative interactions into something positive and empowering.

_____

_____

_____

Excuse 12

I Don't Speak Their Language

EXCUSE BUSTER:

There is more than one way to communicate! Take a risk and go anyway. The language will sort itself out.

Ask:

1. How do you approach new situations—with negative judgment or with an open mind?

   _____

   _____

   _____

2. What steps can you take to handle basic communication in another language?

   _____

   _____

   _____

Action Items:

1. Name a time when language—either a foreign language or a conversation you simply couldn't keep up with—held you back from connecting with someone.

2. What two steps could you take if you're in a similar situation in the future that could turn it into positive experience?

3. How can you communicate with your smile? With your body language? With your eyes?

ACKNOWLEDGMENTS

This section should really be a book unto itself, as this journey has included too many people to count, let alone name. I will do my best, but as I have always said, if I forget to name someone here, you know who you are and have my eternal gratitude.

Nancy L. Erickson was my BOOK PROFESSOR (www. thebookprofessor.com). Nancy served too many roles to count, from editor and coach to teacher and drill sergeant. I could not have done this without you, and if I had, I don't think I would be as happy with it. Thanks for guiding me the whole way.

Thank you to my parents, Joe and Julie, and to my siblings: Lynn, Mark, and Katie. Most of the adventures I wrote about began after we all moved out of the house, but you all provided the foundation! Here's to sharing more adventures together with our growing families! Speaking of family, thank you to my 'big brother' and cousin, David, and all of our amazing relatives.

A decade in entertainment was made possible by a handful of key people. Josh Routh, you are like the Godfather to my career, and I don't think I'll ever be able to return the favor in full (Ginger Routh, thank you for Josh and everything you both do as well!). Thanks also to Jeff Lefton, Dan Sims, Keith Robinson, Elizabeth Austin, Teddy Burke, and everyone involved with Circus Kaput, Complete Music, and Abra-Kid-Abra.

Thank you everyone involved with The JET Program and every travel buddy along the way: Yuji Higuchi, Tracy Whiting Kiper, Kinuko Murayama and family, Ed Snook, Treve Brinkman, Brenna Dorrance, Kelly Norris, Ben Colbridge, the Kumamoto Hashers, Ryota "Yoda" Tsuno, Toshi, Leti & Paco.

These incredible folks have provided knowledge, insight, and inspiration about speaking and running a business: Patrick Combs, Josh Shipp, Shep Hyken, David Fisher, Duane Hixon, Patrick McLaughlin, Marty Domitrovich, Jason Wians, Quain Tull, and all of my friends over the years in Vector/Cutco, YSU, and a multitude of successful small business owners.

A few noteworthy people were instrumental in starting my speaking career: Among many: Maria Palumbo, Andy Mayer, Jenny Armbruster and everyone at the NCADA, Amanda Penicks and everyone at 4-H, Rick Danzeisen, Caitlin Ebel, Justin and Jennifer Donald, Janie Strebeck, Jeff Baker, Katie Rengel, Maddy Reigel, and special thanks to Ted "Mr. Frig" Frigillana for all your support, encouragement, and friendship.

Several friends were mentioned in this book, including members of the "Fab Five" at Loyola: Katie, Josh, Sal, and Liz. Other influences and friends from good times at Loyola, SLUH, and beyond include Eric Fitts, Michelle Brecht, John Gotway, Dave Marlo, Michelle Brecht, Craig Hannick, Peggy Quinn, Dr. Tai, Dr. Gavin, Jerry Overbeck, Sara Koeper, Molly Kelly, Erica Balven.

To Mark and the Garvey clan, along with the entire Corpus Christi community, you will always hold a special place in my heart.

I have achieved my destiny in life: I'm a Dad. Hiroki and Amane, I hope I can live a life that inspires you to love yours. Thank you for your constant hugs, smiles, and joy.

Finally, I could not even fathom pursuing this crazy ride of life without the greatest wife, mom, and travel partner in the world. Michiyo, you had no idea what you were in for, but your support, understanding, patience, and love are the reasons for any level of my success and happiness. Thank you for loving me and saying yes. 愛してる!!!

ABOUT THE AUTHOR

Joe Fingerhut rocks audiences across America and around the world as a sought-after inspirational speaker. He shares stories of global travel and dream jobs from over two decades of adventure to entertain, inspire and empower.

As a speaker, Joe is passionate about inspiring young people to dream bigger dreams, to eliminate obstacles, and be their own leader themselves, all the while teaching them the power of right choices, attitude, and character. Joe is an international speaker at schools, conferences, universities, and corporate events.

Joe and Michiyo have two bilingual, perfect little angels, Hiroki and Amane. Their family resides in St. Louis and spends part of the year in Kumamoto, Japan, where they enjoy onsen, hanami, and sashimi, kotatsu, and eating with chopsticks.

To learn more about Joe and book him for your next event, visit www.joefingerhut.com.